D·U·B·L·I·N·E·R·S
A PLURALISTIC WORLD

Twayne's Masterwork Studies
Robert Lecker, General Editor

D·U·B·L·I·N·E·R·S
A PLURALISTIC WORLD

CRAIG HANSEN WERNER

TWAYNE PUBLISHERS • BOSTON
A DIVISION OF G. K. HALL & CO.

Dubliners: A Pluralistic World
Craig Hansen Werner

Twayne's Masterwork Studies No. 20

Copyright 1988 by G. K. Hall & Co.
All rights reserved.
Published by Twayne Publishers
A Division of G. K. Hall & Co.
70 Lincoln Street
Boston, Massachusetts 02111

Copyediting supervised by Barbara Sutton
Book production by Gabrielle B. McDonald

Typeset in 10/14 Sabon
by Compset, Inc., Beverly, Massachusetts

Printed on permanent/durable acid-free paper
and bound in the United States of America

Library of Congress Cataloging–in–Publication Data

Werner, Craig Hansen, 1952–
    Dubliners : a pluralistic world / Craig Hansen Werner.
        p.   cm.—(Twayne's masterwork studies ; no. 20)
    Bibliography: p.
    Includes index.
    ISBN 0-8057-7970-1 (alk. paper).   ISBN 0-8057-8021-1 (pbk. : alk.
paper)
    1. Joyce, James, 1882–1941.   Dubliners.   2. Dublin (Dublin) in
literature.   I. Title.   II. Series.
PR6019.09D885   1988
823'.912—dc19   88-5241
                                                                 CIP

CONTENTS

NOTE ON REFERENCES
AND ACKNOWLEDGMENTS

All citations of *Dubliners* are from the Viking Compass edition, which incorporates Robert Scholes's textual corrections. Every widely available edition of *Dubliners* uses the Scholes text. Because of the large number of texts available for specific stories (many of which are frequently anthologized), I have elected not to include page references in the text. References to specific works of criticism are noted in the text. Full publication information is available in the Bibliography.

The spelling of the name Stephen Daedalus/Dedalus varies as such throughout this book because Joyce changed his mind about the spelling between *Stephen Hero* (which uses the former, classical spelling) and *A Portrait of the Artist as a Young Man* (which uses the latter spelling).

Any critic working on James Joyce owes an immense debt to the many individuals who have provided essential information and explored some of the potential pathways to Joyce's work. While I have attempted to identify the most influential of these critics (particularly in Chapter 3), I would like to single out for special thanks Florence Walzl, whose work on *Dubliners* over three decades establishes a standard of excellence for all later critics. Bernard Benstock has encouraged my interest in things Joycean since my graduate student days at the University of Illinois. Specific support for this project has been provided by the Research Committee of the Graduate School and by the Institute for Research in the Humanities at the University of Wisconsin-Madison. I would like to express my thanks to my wife, Leslee Nelson, and my daughter, Riah Wakenda Werner. Finally, I wish to dedicate this book to Barbara Talmadge, who always wanted me to be a Joycean.

Adam and Eve Church, Dublin.
Photograph by Christine Bond.
© 1987 by Christine Bond. Used by permission.

CHRONOLOGY: JAMES JOYCE'S LIFE AND WORKS

1882	Birth of James Joyce on Groundhog Day, 2 February, a coincidence the writer loved. The first of ten children born to John Stanislaus and Mary (Murray) Joyce. Intensely proud of the family heritage, John Joyce imparted to his son a gift for storytelling, a tendency toward excessive drinking, and an inability to cope with finances. Unlike her anticlerical husband, May Joyce was a devout Catholic whom James remembered as a source of unshakable love.
1888	Enters Clongowes Wood College, County Kildare. Although Joyce was to reject most of the specific teachings of his Jesuit masters, he maintained a high level of respect for their intellectual rigor.
1889	Fall of Charles Stewart Parnell, leader of the Irish Home Rule movement. Parnell's death in 1891 inspired Joyce's first literary production, a satirical poem titled "Et Tu, Healy," which his father distributed to friends.
1892	John Joyce loses his position at the Rates Office, accelerating the economic decline that forced a series of moves to less comfortable living quarters that would continue throughout Joyce's youth.
1893	Brief enrollment in the Christian Brothers' School of Dublin, which Joyce disliked and rarely mentioned. Subsequently enters Belvedere College, a Jesuit day school, where he received basic training in Latin, French, and Italian. Begins to take the long walks that provide the base of his encyclopedic knowledge of Dublin geography.
1896	Chosen prefect of the Sodality of the Blessed Virgin Mary at Belvedere. Probably experiences first sexual encounter. Begins work on *Silhouettes*, a series of prose sketches, and *Moods*, a book of poems. The association of religious fervor, sensuality,

and creative inspiration recurs throughout Joyce's published work.

1898   Enters University College, Dublin, the Jesuit alternative to the prestigious, but Protestant, Trinity College. As his family's economic condition worsens, Joyce begins aesthetic discussions with friends. It was probably during 1898 when Joyce stopped considering himself a Catholic. When questioned later as to when he left the Church, he would respond "That is for the church to say."

1899   Following riots over *The Countess Cathleen,* Joyce defends Yeats's play against Catholic and nationalist criticism.

1900   Defense of Ibsen's drama inspires vociferous debate at University College. Review of *When We Dead Awaken* published in the *Fortnightly Review* elicits a letter of thanks from Ibsen. Begins work on the sketches that will develop into his "epiphanies" and writes an Ibsenesque play, *A Brilliant Career.*

1901   Writing to Ibsen on his seventy-third birthday, Joyce cryptically announces his own imminent appearance on the stage of European letters. "Day of the Rabblement," Joyce's broadside condemning the Irish Literary Theatre for narrow nationalism, is privately printed.

1902   Direct contact with the Irish literary movement, particularly George Russell (AE), Yeats, and Lady Gregory. Although parts of the story are apocryphal, Joyce was widely believed to have told Yeats on their first meeting, "You are too old for me to help you." Leaves for Paris on 1 December, ostensibly to continue medical studies begun at Royal University Medical School in Dublin. Returning home for Christmas, he meets Oliver St. John Gogarty, the model for Buck Mulligan in *Ulysses.*

1903   Returns from Paris to Dublin in April after receiving a telegram announcing his mother's imminent death, which occurs on 13 August. Asserting his independence, Joyce refuses to honor her deathbed wish that he take communion.

1904   Earliest version of "A Portrait of the Artist." Begins work on *Stephen Hero* and the poems collected in *Chamber Music.* On 16 June—the date on which *Ulysses* takes place—Joyce has his first extended meeting with Nora Barnacle, his future wife. "The Sisters," the first of three stories from *Dubliners* to be published in the *Irish Homestead,* is published on 13 August. In October, Joyce and Nora leave for the Continent where he teaches English at the Berlitz school in Pola (then in Austria, now in Yugoslavia).

1905   Moves to the Berlitz school in Trieste, an Austrian port city (now part of Italy) with Italian traditions and sympathies. On 27 July, Nora gives birth to a son, Giorgio. Stanislaus Joyce, who would be instrumental, if largely unappreciated, in providing financial and intellectual support, joins his brother's family in Trieste. Joyce finishes work on the original version of *Dubliners*, which he sends to publisher Grant Richards on 3 December.

1906   On 17 February, Grant Richards accepts *Dubliners* for publication. By mid-April, Joyce and Richards are deeply engaged in a series of battles over censorship and revision that result in ongoing legal problems. Joyce moves to Rome, which he despises, and works in a bank.

1907   Returns to Trieste, where Joyce becomes friends with Ettore Schmitz (Italo Svevo). Finishes writing "The Dead." On 26 July, a daughter, Lucia, is born.

1908   Continuing problems concerning *Dubliners*, which is rejected by numerous publishers.

1909   Joyce and Giorgio visit Ireland, staying in Dublin and in Galway with Nora's relatives. Vincent Cosgrave's (probably unfounded) claim that Nora betrayed Joyce several years earlier initiates a period of marital difficulty. On 19 August, Joyce signs a contract with Maunsel & Co. for publication of *Dubliners*. After bringing his sister Eva to Trieste, Joyce returns to Dublin in October to establish the first Irish cinema in partnership with several Triestine businessmen.

1910   Returns to Trieste along with another sister, Eileen. Throughout the Trieste period, Stanislaus provides the majority of financial support for the growing Joyce clan. George Roberts, overseeing publication of *Dubliners* for Maunsel, raises new objections to the manuscript.

1911   In despair over the continued delays, Joyce sends an open letter to the Irish press concerning the history of *Dubliners*.

1912   Lectures on William Blake and Daniel Defoe. Makes final visit to Ireland along with Nora and children. Problems with Roberts over *Dubliners* continue, leading to burning of the sheets on 11 September.

1913   Receives letter from Ezra Pound, who will play a central role in furthering his career.

1914   Grant Richards agrees to publish *Dubliners*, which appears on 15 June to generally enthusiastic notice, but few sales. Writes *Giacomo Joyce*, an impressionistic memoir of an unrequited love affair. With Pound's encouragement, begins associations with longtime patron Harriet Weaver and with *Egoist* editor Dora Marsden, who accepts *A Portrait of the Artist as a Young Man* for serial publication. Begins work on the play *Exiles* and on *Ulysses*.

1915   Arrives in Zurich, the family's primary residence throughout the Great War. A perhaps apocryphal story claims that Joyce met Lenin, who was in exile prior to the Russian Revolution.

1916   Joyce's teaching income is supplemented by various gifts and a Civil List grant attained with the help of Yeats. Several friends and relatives are killed during the Easter Rising in Dublin. Overcoming renewed problems with printers, B. W. Huebsch publishes *A Portrait of the Artist as a Young Man* in New York in December.

1917   The first of many eye operations. Harriet Weaver begins the regular patronage that provides the basis of Joyce's financial security for the rest of his life.

1918   The *Little Review* begins serial publication of *Ulysses*. *Exiles* published on 25 May. Mrs. Harold McCormick makes a substantial financial gift to Joyce. Meets Frank Budgen, the most intimate friend of his later years. Joyce's involvement with the English Players theatrical company results in the lawsuit on which Tom Stoppard's play *Travesties* is based. Infatuation with Marthe Fleischmann commands much of his attention for several months.

1919   *Exiles* premieres in Munich. Concerned with reports of Joyce's heavy drinking, Mrs. McCormick withdraws her patronage. In October, Joyce and his family return to Trieste.

1920   Under Pound's influence, the Joyces move to Paris, where Joyce completes work on *Ulysses*. Meets Sylvia Beach who will be instrumental in the book's publication. The United States government confiscates and burns issues of the *Little Review* containing episodes of *Ulysses*.

1921   *Little Review* convicted for publishing obscenity. Beach and Weaver arrange for book publication of *Ulysses*. Valery Larbaud's 7 December lecture marks culmination of support from Parisian literary community.

1922   Joyce receives first copy of *Ulysses* on his birthday. Foundation of the Irish Free State, which Joyce interprets as the political analogue of his own freeing of the Irish literary consciousness.

1923   Problems with eyes and teeth worsen. On 11 March, begins work on *Finnegans Wake*, which he conceives as a night book balancing the day book of *Ulysses*.

1924   Sections of *Finnegans Wake* begin to appear in the *transatlantic review* and other periodicals under the title "Work in Progress."

1925   Several more eye operations.

1926   First English production of *Exiles*. Meets Eugene and Maria Jolas, whose review *transition* will publish several sections of "Work in Progress."

1927   Letter of protest issued concerning the pirating of an American edition of *Ulysses* by Samuel Roth. *Pomes Penyeach* published on 7 July. Joyce quarrels with Pound and Wyndham Lewis over literary matters.

1928   Work on French translation of *Ulysses* initiates Joyce's friendship with Stuart Gilbert, whom he encourages to write a critical study of *Ulysses*.

1929   Samuel Beckett is among the contributors to a book of essays on "Work in Progress" overseen by Joyce. Nora undergoes hysterectomy. Joyce begins somewhat obsessive support of Irish tenor John Sullivan.

1930   Returns to Zurich for additional operations on eyes. Meets Paul Leopold, who proves indispensable in handling Joyce's correspondence and daily business for most of the rest of his life. Joyce encourages Herbert Gorman to write a biography.

1931   Joyce and Nora are married on 4 July. Joyce's father dies on 29 December, casting Joyce into an extended depression.

1932   Bennet Cerf at Random House contracts with Joyce for an American edition of *Ulysses,* agreeing to undertake necessary legal action. Joyce declines Yeats's invitation to become a charter member of the Academy of Irish Letters. Sparked partially by her unrequited love for Beckett, a frequent visitor in the Joyce household, Lucia begins to suffer from the schizophrenia that commands much of Joyce's attention during the last decade of his life. Giorgio's wife, Helen, gives birth to a son, Stephen, named after Joyce's fictional alter ego.

1933   With Joyce's support, Budgen publishes *James Joyce and the Making of "Ulysses"*. Judge John M. Woolsey issues landmark decision admitting *Ulysses* into the United States.

1934   Lucia's institutionalization becomes inevitable. Joyce devotes much of the next several years to seeking alternative locations and potential cures for her mental illness.

1936   Joyce visits Copenhagen to pay tribute to Ibsen. First British publication of *Ulysses*.

1937   Final meeting with Harriet Weaver, whom Joyce unjustly accuses of having withheld support from Lucia and himself.

1938   Although he professes general disinterest in political events, Joyce aids several people, including novelist Hermann Broch, in their escape from Nazi territory. Finishes work on *Finnegans Wake*.

1939   Publication of *Finnegans Wake* celebrated at Joyce's birthday party on 2 February. Official publication on 4 May. Corrects galley proofs of Gorman's biography, leading to several biographical misconceptions. Attempts to relocate family away from Paris.

1940   Lives briefly under German occupation in French countryside after fall of Paris. With aid of Paul Leon, corrects misprints in *Finnegans Wake*. On 17 December, the Joyce family finally succeeds in reaching Zurich.

1941   Dies of a perforated ulcer on 13 January following a brief hospitalization.

Flats, Crompton Court, Dublin.
Photograph by Christine Bond.
© 1987 by Christine Bond. Used by permission.

· 1 ·

HISTORICAL CONTEXT

James Joyce began his career as an Irishman with his eyes turned toward Europe. Once he arrived on the Continent, his vision returned insistently to his native island. Any understanding of Joyce's response to the complex political and aesthetic dislocations of his era requires an awareness of the specifically Irish manifestations of the larger cultural forces that shaped modernism. As Joyce was well aware, Ireland experienced the major movements of the nineteenth century—particularly the industrial revolution and the emergence of political nationalism—from the marginal perspective of a conquered province. Like his father, Joyce attributed Ireland's economic and psychological malaise to a combination of English oppression and Irish self-betrayal. Similarly, the new currents in continental aesthetics that provided basic materials for his unique version of modernism reached Joyce through the mediation of the Irish Literary Renaissance.

The tension between the devout maternal and the anticlerical paternal branches of his family instilled in Joyce an intense awareness of Irish politics, which he saw as inseparable from Irish Catholicism. Grounded in profound cultural differences and ancient racial antagonism, the historical animosity between Irish and English provides the central motif of Irish history from the Norman Conquest to the present. From the Irish perspective, England has always appeared in the role of arrogant conqueror, devoted to economic exploitation and cultural imposition. To a large extent, the facts—repeated economic depression, abusive absentee landlords, devastating famines, the absence of effective political representation—bear out the Irish complaints.

Not surprisingly, given his father's intense nationalism, Joyce shows a high awareness of the heroes of the various Irish independence movements: Robert Emmet, a romantic rebel executed in 1803; parliamentary nationalist Daniel O'Connell, known as "the Liberator"; Fenian leader Michael Davitt; and, above all, Joyce's childhood hero, Charles Stewart Parnell, "uncrowned king" of the Irish Home Rule movement and focal point of "Ivy Day in the Committee Room." During the 1880s the Home Rule movement gathered sufficient strength in the English parliament to force the resignation of Prime Minister William Gladstone. At the peak of Parnell's power in 1890, however, it was revealed that he had engaged in an extramarital liaison with the wife of an Irish officer, who had tolerated the affair for nearly a decade. Denounced by the Irish clergy and abandoned by many of his supporters, Parnell withdrew from public life. Deprived of its symbolic center, the Home Rule movement collapsed in disarray. Parnell died less than a year later, reinforcing Joyce's belief that the English could count on the Irish to enforce their own oppression through clerical collaboration and political self-betrayal.

Whatever the origins of the problem, the Dublin of Joyce's youth was a severely depressed economic environment, a fact brought home by the continuing decline of the Joyce family fortunes. A sequence of widely resented English laws and trade policies had kept Ireland in a state of depression through most of the nineteenth century. The Famine of 1845—which lasted for nearly half a decade and was immeasurably worsened by a typhus epidemic—remained the symbol of the impact of English rule on Irish life. The effects of the famine were by no means symbolic, however. Between 1845 and 1851, an estimated one million Irish died of famine-related causes; another million left the country. The majority relocated in the United States, which became a center of support for Irish nationalism. To a great extent, Ireland had not recovered from the famine by the end of the century. Both unemployment and income statistics show Ireland lagging far behind England and most of the industrializing Continent. The absence of economic opportunity in turn exerted a major influence on the social customs that Joyce describes in *Dubliners,* which is inhabited by a large number of un- or underemployed young men. Perhaps the most telling statistic related to Ireland's economic woes concerns marriage rates. Unable to support families, Irish men delayed marriage to unusually late ages; in 1911 over seventy percent of men between twenty-five and thirty-five were unmarried, by far the highest rate in the Western world. As Florence Walzl notes in her fine essay "*Dubliners:* Women in Irish Society," this shapes a social pattern in which men spend most of their time with other men, establishing a pattern continued after marriage. This in turn tends to isolate the women, who develop a tendency—also reflected in *Dubliners*—to become overdependent on their children. Particularly in the case of the male children presented with an image of a separate male world, this frequently generates a strong desire to break away from the maternal influence. Reinforced by the absence of economic opportunity, the sons immerse themselves in male companionship, thereby instituting a new cycle.

While the Irish environment provides the most important context of *Dubliners,* Joyce was also aware of the forces giving rise to a self-consciously "modern" sensibility in Europe. It is practically impossible to define adequately terms such as "modern" or "modernism." The "certainties" of the medieval worldview—the intricately interlocking hierarchies providing a coherent structure for understanding religion, nature, government, human nature, etc.—had been under attack for centuries. Calling into question the idea of an immutable superlunary realm analogous to God's perfect wisdom, Galileo's scientific observations paralleled the theological-political fragmentation of the Reformation. Nonetheless, it seems clear that as the nineteenth century progressed, the emotional and intellectual implications of the gradual historical process began to be felt more forcefully. The unleashing of immense physical power through such inventions as the steam engine and the dynamo radically altered economic and cultural organization, creating an urban proletariat on a previously unimagined scale. In addition, the world accessible to intellectuals was rapidly expanding both spatially, through aggressive geographical exploration, and chronologically, through the discovery of the historical realities of Egypt and Troy, which in turn sparked a wholesale reconsideration of the relationship between myth and history. Darwin challenged scientific-theological orthodoxy; Nietzsche questioned the groundwork of philosophy; new armaments rendered war increasingly devastating. The catalog of dislocations confronted by European culture during the nineteenth century could be extended indefinitely. While Paul Fussell's *The Great War and Modern Memory* argues persuasively that World War I marks the crucial transition to the modernist "waste land," the underlying elements of the shift—the sense of fragmentation, uncertainty, dislocation—were clearly visible in the Dublin of Joyce's youth.

By the time Joyce began to articulate his perceptions, the groundwork for the basic modernist responses to the fragmented world was in place. The key words for modernist aesthetics, certainly for those that influenced Joyce, are "extremity" and "contradiction." In literary terms, these concepts come into focus around the tension between "objective" modes such as realism and naturalism and "subjective" modes such as symbolism and romanticism. Although "realism" assumed numerous guises during the nineteenth century, ranging from Dickens's to Turgenev's to Twain's, the French view of the novelist as a detached observer seems most relevant to Joyce. In "The Experimental Novel" Émile Zola described the novelist as "both observer and experimenter. The observer in him presents data as he has observed them, determines the point of departure, establishes the solid ground on which his characters will stand and his phenomena take place. Then the experimenter appears and institutes the experiment, that is, sets the characters of a particular story in motion, in order to show that the series of events therein will be those demanded by the determinism of the phenomena under study."[1] Later novelists who, like Joyce, resisted Zola's explicit sociological determinism extended realism into more subtle psychological areas. Fascinated by the interaction between internal perception and socioeconomic status, Gustave

Flaubert and Henry James developed prose styles appropriate to their characters' apprehensions of reality. Perhaps the most significant general contribution of realism to Joyce's context, however, was simply that it shifted emphasis from the grand actions of elevated characters to the generally unexceptional events experienced by ordinary individuals. For Joyce, the greatest realist was Danish dramatist Henrik Ibsen, whose penetrating treatments of bourgeois life established a standard of moral integrity and aesthetic excellence against which the younger Irishman would continue to judge his own achievement. A letter written by Flaubert sums up the importance of realism to the developing Joycean aesthetic: "The artist should be in his work like God in creation, invisible and all-powerful; he should be felt everywhere, but he should not be seen."[2]

Complementing this self-consciously "objective" tendency in nineteenth-century literature was an equally influential "subjective" tendency that extended from the romanticism of Blake and Shelley through the symbolists and aesthetes of the 1890s. Stressing the central importance of the individual sensibility to the interpretation and/or creation of reality, the romantics (whose internal disagreements are even more extensive than those of the realists) explored diverse modes of consciousness. For the French symbolists, whose work became known in the English-speaking world largely through Arthur Symons's influential book, *The Symbolist Movement in Literature* (1899), this subjective emphasis—reinforced by the developing field of psychoanalysis—engendered a deep interest in the subconscious mind, mysticism, and dream states. Some writers fascinated with the relationship between individual psychology and its social context—Flaubert is perhaps the best example—attempted to merge the realist and symbolist currents. Nonetheless, both for realists such as Frank Norris and for aesthetes such as Walter Pater, the primary interest continued to be the full development of either the "subjective" or the "objective" approach.

Both currents reached Joyce through the mediation of the Irish Literary Renaissance, a diffuse movement that emerged slowly in the last quarter of the nineteenth century, reaching its peak in Dublin between 1890 and 1920. As a young man, Joyce was acutely aware of the attention attracted by the work of slightly older writers including Douglas Hyde, George Russell (known under his literary name of AE), Lady Gregory, and W. B. Yeats. Most of the Dublin writers were interested primarily in the symbolic current of nineteenth-century aesthetics, inasmuch as it reinforced their interest in the theosophical speculations of Mme Blavatsky and in folk or pseudofolk literary forms. Although Joyce maintained some distance from the major figures of the Irish Literary Renaissance, he shared their interest in the legends and oral traditions that differentiated the Irish sensibility from that of the English. At the same time, Dublin was not without its connection with the realistic temperament. George Moore was well known for his realistic novels, many of which focused on specifically Irish concerns; George Bernard Shaw, though he rarely dealt explicitly with Irish themes, had emerged as a leading figure in the development of a "scientific" modern drama. What all of these writers shared was an uneasy relationship with their native country, a relationship that emerged forcefully during Joyce's formative years. The 1899 production of Yeats's play, *The Countess Cathleen,* was attacked as heretical and/or anti-Irish; similarly, rioting greeted the first production of John Millington Synge's *The Playboy of the Western World* in 1907. These intensely Irish battles reinforced Joyce's sense of the inevitable conflict between the sensitive artist and the narrow social context.

By the time his first works were published, Joyce had left Ireland for the heterogeneous port of Trieste and later the cosmopolitan cultural ferment of Paris. Major modernist artists such as Ezra Pound, Wyndham Lewis, and Valery Larbaud would play significant roles in his post–*Dubliners* intellectual and aesthetic development. Yet the terms of Joyce's encounter with the world were without a doubt established during the two decades he spent in Ireland. Whether in his keen eye for the realistic detail revealing the incoherence of the modern personality or in his ironic sense of the aesthetically refined consciousness as a half-sufficient retreat from the incoherence, Joyce never ceased to reflect the confrontation between the Irish and the modern world.

· 2 ·

THE IMPORTANCE OF THE WORK

James Joyce's first mature work can be appreciated both in its own terms and as a precursor of the author's later masterpieces. An unsparing vision of the "paralysis" that Joyce saw afflicting his native city, *Dubliners* exemplifies the early modernist synthesis of Zola's "scientific objectivity" and the intensely subjective aesthetics associated with symbolist poetry. Combining these apparently antagonistic influences, Joyce developed a number of techniques—most notably the concept of the *epiphany* and the approach to the short story collection as a montage/novel—that have exerted substantial influence over later writers of short fiction. Despite its demonstrable influence, however, *Dubliners* would probably never have attracted more than passing attention if Joyce had not gone on to write *Ulysses* and *Finnegans Wake*. As a result, discussions of the book's importance frequently, and sometimes overingenuously, focus on *Dubliners* as the source for a multitude of thematic concerns and rhetorical devices exploited fully in its encyclopedic successors.

Although the position of *Dubliners* in literary history derives primarily from Joyce's later work, its influence requires no external explanation. The technique Joyce referred to as the *epiphany* and his insistence on the short story collection as a unified entity establish Joyce alongside Anton Chekhov as a central figure in the development of twentieth-century short fiction. Like Chekhov's pointedly realistic sketches of nineteenth-century Russian society, Joyce's stories immerse the reader in a dense texture of realistic detail that both reflects and comments on his characters' experience of their specific social milieu. Defined in *Stephen Hero* as "a sudden spiritual manifestation, whether in the vulgarity of speech or of gesture or in a memorable phase of the mind itself," the concept of the epiphany has been explored by numerous writers seeking the articulate both mundane external ("the vulgarity of speech or of gesture") and rarified internal ("a memorable phase of the mind itself") experiences. While Henry James, Ernest Hemingway, Thomas Mann, Virginia Woolf, and others contributed to the psychological synthesis of romanticism and realism, the Joycean epiphany—which can be used with various degrees of irony accessible to either character or reader—exerts a clear influence on writers as diverse as Gabriel García Márquez, Samuel Beckett, Richard Wright, Ann Beattie, and Jayne Anne Phillips.

The second major contribution of *Dubliners* concerns its overall structure. In part because most nineteenth-century short stories were intended for publication in periodicals, they were usually conceived as self-contained units. When collected in book form, they might be loosely tied together by setting (Chekhov's *In the Steppes*), mood (Poe's *Tales of the Grotesque and Arabesque*), or character (Joel Chandler Harris's *Uncle Remus, His Songs and Sayings*). Prior to *Dubliners,* however, few were conceived (and even fewer recognized) as works with the structural and thematic coherence usually associated with novels. Almost from the time he began writing stories for publication in the *Irish Homestead* newspaper, Joyce seems to have envisioned their place in the larger structure of *Dubliners.* Involving image patterns, thematic variations, and a careful positioning of stories, his structural experiment anticipates modernist experiments with "montage form" such as Sherwood Anderson's *Winesburg, Ohio*, Hemingway's *In Our Time*, William Faulkner's *Go Down, Moses* and Wright's *Uncle Tom's Children.* As the influence of these writers mingled with that of *Dubliners,* most readers, particularly those in the United States, began to assume the underlying unity found in collections as diverse as Ernest Gaines's *Bloodline,* Jayne Anne Phillips's *Black Tickets,* Guy Davenport's *DaVinci's Bicycle,* and Flannery O'Connor's *Everything That Rises Must Converge.*

As influential as the techniques of the synthesizing epiphany and the short story montage/novel have proven to be, neither was unique to Joyce. If Joyce had not written *Dubliners,* it is doubtful that the shape of twentieth-century short fiction would have been radically altered. The actual impact of the volume, however, cannot be divorced from the immense impact of Joyce's later work. As accomplished as the stories are, they were read by many—including other writers— only after encounters with *Ulysses* or *Finnegans Wake.* As a result, *Dubliners* has frequently been read as a precursor of the later works, a tendency with both benefits and dangers. On the one hand, familiarity with "Dubliners" such as Martin Cunningham ("Grace") and Corley and Lenehan ("Two Gallants") enriches appreciation of their appearances in *Ulysses.* Familiarity with specific motifs in the early stories—the guilt associated with sexual perversion in "An Encounter" or the disillusioned romanticism of "Araby"—can help clarify otherwise obscure passages in *Finnegans Wake.* While it seems legitimate to read the later works with an awareness of the earlier, there is a distinct danger of overreading the early stories by assuming (explicitly or otherwise) that Joyce always had his full-life's work clearly in mind. Critical exercises such as the uncovering of detailed Homeric parallels and multivalent puns in *Dubliners,* while not necessarily invalid, frequently obscure the unique achievement of Joyce's early work.

Not merely a function of literary history, that achievement rests on the power of the individual stories and of *Dubliners* as a whole. Several stories, among them "Araby," "Two Gallants," and "The Dead," have assumed independent lives in anthologies of English literature or the short-story genre. "The Dead," with its complex rendering of the psychological texture of the Conroy marriage, ranks with the finest fiction of any era. Combined with his sharp eye for the luminous detail, Joyce's complex balancing of sympathy and irony confronts readers with an exceptionally challenging image of the economic, psychological, and cultural dislocations of the modernist era. Although Joyce would explore diverse aspects of this dilemma in greater depth in his later work, *Dubliners* remains his most accessible articulation of the central problems of the "unexceptional" individual in the modern world.

· 3 ·

CRITICAL RECEPTION

What has been made of James Joyce is almost as important as what Joyce made. In part, this reflects the density of his prose, even the *relatively* accessible prose of *Dubliners*. In part, however, it reflects Joyce's conscious decision to assume the role of his own first critic. Conditioned initially by the hesitation of printers and publishers—which Joyce interpreted as censorship—and later by the emergence of a burgeoning "James Joyce industry," criticism of *Dubliners* has passed through phases of naturalism and symbolism to the contemporary emphasis on the interrelationship of style, theme, and the larger forces conditioning both.

Anticipating an approach he was to refine into a minor art form in his comments on *Ulysses* and *Finnegans Wake*, Joyce issued a number of pronouncements and scattered a variety of hints concerning his intentions in *Dubliners*. The clearest of Joyce's statements occurs in a letter of 5 May 1906 to Grant Richards, who was then considering publishing the volume. Identifying both the thematic and structural centers of *Dubliners*, Joyce wrote: "My intention was to write a chapter of the moral history of my country and I chose Dublin for the scene because that city seemed to me the centre of paralysis. I have tried to present it to the indifferent public under four of its aspects: childhood, adolescence, maturity and public life. The stories are arranged in this order. I have written it for the most part in a style of scrupulous meanness and with the conviction that he is a very bold man who dares to alter in the presentment, still more to deform, whatever he has seen and heard."[3] The emphasis on paralysis; on the book as a gradually expanding unified work; and, to a lesser extent, on the "scrupulous meanness" of Joyce's style have all become leitmotivs of subsequent critical discussion of the book.

Joyce's comments to Richards occurred in the very specific context of his attempts to get the book published. In fact, the earliest critics of *Dubliners* were the editors and printers who seem to have shared a feeling that the book was in some sense obscene or dangerous. Under the laws of the time, both publishers and printers could be held responsible for the contents of any libelous materials produced in association with their businesses. As a result, shortly after Richards accepted the early version of Joyce's manuscript in February 1906, problems emerged that would delay the book's publication for nearly a decade. Richard Ellmann has recounted the tangled story of objections—most of which seem quite trivial in retrospect—Joycean responses, renewed objections from potential publisher George Russell, and Joycean counterobjections. What seems most significant in regard to the eventual reception of *Dubliners* is that Joyce consistently defended his stories on essentially realistic grounds, arguing that he could not change his presentation without distorting the reality of which he wrote. His 23 June 1906 letter to Richards reflects both the tone and content of his position: "It is not my fault that the odour of ashpits and old weeds and offal hangs round my stories. I seriously believe that you will retard the course of civilisation in Ireland by preventing the Irish people from having one good look at themselves in my nicely polished looking glass."[4] While Joyce's letters to Richards include his most influential statements on *Dubliners*, David Jones has identified a number of additional authorial comments in "Approaches to *Dubliners:* Joyce's" (1978). On occasion, the "Aeolus" chapter of *Ulysses,* which includes Stephen Dedalus's *Dubliners*–style sketch

"The Parable of the Plums," has been cited as additional evidence concerning Joyce's early aesthetic. The other significant prepublication critic of *Dubliners* was Stanislaus, Joyce's younger brother and intellectual foil, whose observations were published only during the 1950s. Stanislaus's comments on the stories as they were being written, complemented by the help he provided in verifying the accuracy of various details of Dublin life, were instrumental in helping Joyce refine his realism in theory and practice.

When *Dubliners* was finally published in 1914—ironically under the supervision of Richards, who had changed publishing houses in the interim—it attracted generally positive, if somewhat limited, response. Like nearly all commentary prior to the emergence of an academic Joycean community, the responses accepted Joyce's implicit definition of the book as essentially realistic. Joyce's most influential early critic, Ezra Pound, placed *Dubliners* in the Flaubert tradition of realism. Echoing the "imagist" poetic aesthetic he was then developing, Pound praised the book's "clear hard prose," its ability to give "the thing as it is."[5] Rather than pursuing the implications of Pound's 1914 essay, however, critics shifted their attention to what were then perceived almost universally as the more complex aesthetic explorations of *A Portrait of the Artist as a Young Man* and *Ulysses*, both of which were being published in serial form. As a result, most comments on *Dubliners* over the next two decades treated the book as, in Edmund Wilson's words, a "straight work of naturalistic fiction."[6] Developing this position in more rigorous form, Harry Levin established the premises of Anglo-American criticism on *Dubliners* in his influential book *James Joyce* (1941), still one of the best introductions to the author's overall achievement. Accepting Joyce's identification of paralysis as the thematic center, Levin presents *Dubliners* as the primary statement of the author's concern with external reality. Titling his discussion "The City"—his chapter on *Portrait* is titled "The Artist"—Levin states that Joyce is primarily "concerned with the routines of every-day life, the mechanisms of human behavior." Levin draws the connection between theme and style, adding that Joyce is "anxious to discover the most economical way of exposing the most considerable amount of that material."[7] This leads to an emphasis on the importance of the epiphany, especially in "The Dead," which Levin identifies as the crucial transition to the psychological explorations of *Portrait* and *Ulysses*. In *The Novel and the Modern World* (1939), David Daiches develops a parallel approach to "The Dead" in greater detail. Contrasting "The Dead" with the dominant naturalistic mode of *Dubliners*, Daiches argues that only the final story is presented "in a way that implies comment." This reflects Joyce's decision to "deliberately [allow] his style to surrender, as it were, to that comment, so that the level objectivity of the other stories is replaced by a more lyrical quality."[8] Probably the most comprehensive presentation of the realistic approach, Hugh Kenner's discussion of *Dubliners* in *Dublin's Joyce* (1956) combines the emphasis on "undented verity that controls these stories" with a detailed discussion of the structural development through stages of childhood, maturity, adolescence, and public life. One of the first critics to identify stories other than "The Dead" as central to Joyce's strategy, Kenner singles out "The Sisters" and "A Painful Case" for detailed examination.

While the realist approach clearly dominated early readings of *Dubliners*, an alternative perspective, reflecting the developing emphasis on "close reading" of Joyce's later books, made its first appearance during the 1940s. In their anthology *Understanding Fiction* (1943), widely viewed as the central text of the New Criticism that would dominate American critical practice for three decades, Robert Penn Warren and Cleanth Brooks discussed "Araby" in a manner almost diametrically opposed to the underlying premises of the realist readings. Focusing on internal symbolic patterns with minimal reference to contextual information, Brooks and Warren concluded that "the story is not merely an account of a stage in the process of growing up it does not merely represent a clinical interest in the psychology of growing up—but is a symbolic rendering of a central conflict in mature experience."[9] This emphasis on symbolic and universal—as opposed to personal or local—meaning recurs in Richard Levin and Charles Shattuck's essay "First Flight to Ithaca: A New Reading of Joyce's *Dubliners*" (1947). Like Warren and Brooks, Levin and Shattuck wrote under the obvious influence of T. S. Eliot's "Ulysses, Order, and Myth" (1923), the first essay to celebrate Joyce's "mythic method," his conscious manipulation of "a continuous parallel between contemporaneity and antiquity."[10] Seeking the universal substructure of Joyce's Dublin materials, Levin and Shattuck detailed specific parallels between the *Odyssey* and *Dubliners*. Although most subsequent critics have found "First Flight to Ithaca" overly imaginative, the essay anticipates numerous later attempts to identify anticipations of *Ulysses* and *Finnegans Wake* beneath the realistic surface of Joyce's first fiction. An equally detailed, and much more convincing, development of the symbolic approach can be found in Brewster Ghiselin's classic essay "The Unity of Joyce's *Dubliners*" (1956). Identifying *Dubliners* as "a sequence of events in a moral drama, an action of the human spirit struggling for survival under peculiar conditions of deprivation," Ghiselin argues that beneath the individual stories lies "one essential history, that of the soul of a people which has confused and weakened its relation to the source of spiritual life."[11] Recognizing that the universal themes manifest themselves in relationship to particular circumstances, Ghiselin contends that the "unity of *Dubliners* is realized, finally, in terms of religious images and ideas, most of them distinctively Christian."[12] Along with the discussions by Kenner and Harry Levin, Ghiselin's essay provided a primary point of reference for the explosion of Joyce studies that was to occur during the 1960s.

Few writers have been honored—or perhaps plagued—by the intensive critical scrutiny accorded Joyce over the last three decades. Inspired in large part by Richard Ellmann's masterful critical biography, *James Joyce* (1959, rev. ed. 1982), critics have examined, reexamined, and examined one another's examinations of practically every paragraph of the major works. Although the amount of commentary pales in comparison to that on the later works, *Dubliners* is no exception. Reference works relevant to the book include Don Gifford's invaluable *Notes for Joyce: "Dubliners" and "Portrait of the Artist"* (1967); Gary Lane's *A Word Index to James Joyce's "Dubliners"* (1972); Wilhelm Fuger's *Concordance to James Joyce's "Dubliners"* (1980); Tetsumaro Hayashi's *James Joyce: Research Opportunities and Dissertation Abstracts* (1985), which summarizes over a dozen dissertations devoted specifically to *Dubliners;* Robert Deming's *A*

Bibliography of James Joyce Studies (2d ed. 1977) and *James Joyce: The Critical Heritage* (two vols. 1970); the relevant volume of the massive *James Joyce Archive;* and Thomas Jackson Rice's *James Joyce: A Guide to Research* (1982), the best starting point for research on a particular story or topic. This reference material serves as a massive appendix to the equally massive amount of commentary on both the volume as a whole and on the individual stories. Deming's *Bibliography* catalogs twenty-six commentaries on "Ivy Day in the Committee Room," twenty-eight on "Clay," thirty-six on "Araby," and seventy on "The Dead." The flood has diminished only slightly during the intervening decade. Crucial forums for the emerging Joyce industry, which rivals that concerning any other writer with the possible exception of Shakespeare, have been provided by the *James Joyce Quarterly,* edited by Thomas Staley at the University of Tulsa; the James Joyce Foundation, a professional organization that has played an instrumental role in organizing the popular biannual James Joyce Symposia, which have been held in Joycean locations such as Dublin, Trieste, Paris, and Zurich; and more recently the *James Joyce Literary Supplement,* edited by Bernard Benstock at the University of Miami.

During the early days of the Joyce industry, discussion of *Dubliners* centered on the battle between symbol hunters and a variety of opponents. The groundwork for these battles had been provided by the major statements of the 1940s and 1950s and by Marvin Magalaner's *Time of Apprenticeship: The Fiction of Young James Joyce* (1959). Complemented by Ellmann's biography and Robert Scholes and Richard Kain's sourcebook, *The Workshop of Daedalus* (1965), Magalaner's book provides a fairly comprehensive summary of the backgrounds and composition of the book. Although a handful of books focused specifically on *Dubliners* (sometimes in conjunction with *Portrait*), the most intense battles took place in sequences of essays devoted to individual stories. Perhaps the most heated, and in many ways typical, of these exchanges concerned "Araby." Extending the symbolic emphasis of Ghiselin's essay, Harry Stone's "'Araby' and the Writings of James Joyce" (1965) catalogs structurally and thematically significant allusions to Mary, Queen of Scots, Yeats's "Our Lady of the Hills," Mangan's "Dark Rosaleen," the Irish adultress Caroline

Norton, the obscure theological writer Abednego Sellers, the sensational criminal Vidoq, and a host of other liturgical and literary figures. Although it was generally compatible with the decade's most influential academic readings of *Ulysses,* Stone's analysis attracted the wrath of Robert ApRoberts, whose rejoinder "'Araby' and the Palimpsest of Criticism" (1966) angrily dismisses almost all of Stone's claims. Arguing that Stone's primary flaw is "his basic assumption that 'Araby' is not self contained," ApRoberts summarizes the position of most critics who resisted the symbolic approach: "symbolisms which run counter to the central idea, are discordant with it, are unrelated to it, or claimed to be concurrent with it but to be perceived only by an understanding of an arcane network of unstated details obliquely connected with it are to be rejected unless evidence is adduced from outside the story to show that the author saw such symbolisms in the story." Performing a service that he would render repeatedly in relation to other stories in *Dubliners,* Bernard Benstock sifted through these divergent positions in "Arabesques: Third Position of Concord" (1967), which provides a model for critics seeking to balance sometimes overingenious claims with a respect for Joyce's artistic ingenuity.

Throughout the 1960s, individual critics argued vociferously in favor of various readings, many of which reflected the dominance of New Critical close reading. A cursory glance at the index of the *James Joyce Quarterly* or the listings in Deming's *Bibliography* reveals a plethora of essays—some highly insightful—on topics such as "The Trinity in Joyce's 'Grace'" (Joseph Baker, 1965), "The Crucifixion in 'The Boarding House'" (Bruce Rosenberg, 1967), and "*Dubliners:* Joyce's Dantean Vision" (Warren Carrier, 1965). Contrasting with such symbolic readings were "common sense" statements such as that of S. L. Goldberg, whose 1962 book on Joyce emphasizes the "relative immaturity" of the author at the time he wrote *Dubliners.* Taken to its extreme, the common-sense attitude resulted in explications such as those included in Warren Beck's book *Joyce's "Dubliners": Substance, Vision, and Art* (1969) which in effect throws the baby out with the bathwater, refusing to accept any dimension of meaning not immediately evident.

Considered retrospectively, the greatest contribution of the Joyce explosion of the 1960s lies in the cumulative clarification of individual stories. Almost every story in *Dubliners* has been dealt with sensitively on at least one occasion. A partial listing of essays worth the attention of the contemporary student of *Dubliners* would include Benstock's "'The Sisters' and the Critics" (1966), Father Robert Boyle's "'Two Gallants' and 'Ivy Day in the Committee Room'" (1963), Florence Walzl's "Gabriel and Michael: The Conclusion of 'The Dead'" (1966), John William Corrington's "Isolation as Motif in 'A Painful Case'" (1966), and the chapters by David Hayman ("A Mother") and Zack Bowen ("After the Race") in Clive Hart's anthology *James Joyce's "Dubliners": Critical Essays* (1969). As a composite reading of *Dubliners*, Hart's anthology is far more satisfactory than the single-author explications by Magalaner, Beck, Epifanio San Juan (*James Joyce and the Craft of Fiction*, 1972), Edward Brandabur (*A Scrupulous Meanness*, 1971), or, more recently, Donald Torchiana (*Backgrounds for Joyce's "Dubliners,"* 1986). The appearance of Hart's anthology, along with several collections of previously published material (William Moynihan's *James Joyce's "The Dead,"* 1965; Peter Garrett's *Twentieth Century Interpretations of "Dubliners,"* 1968; James Baker and Thomas Staley's *James Joyce's "Dubliners": A Critical Handbook,* 1969; Robert Scholes and A. Walton Litz's *James Joyce's "Dubliners": Text, Criticism and Notes,* 1969; and Morris Beja's *James Joyce, "Dubliners," and "A Portrait of the Artist as a Young Man,"* 1973) mark the end of the first major outburst of *Dubliners* criticism. Collectively, these anthologies helped identify "canonical" early essays (Ghiselin, Kenner) and began sifting through the more recent work, focusing attention on the consistently valuable work of experienced critics such as Boyle and Walzl, whose chapter in *A Companion to Joyce Studies* (ed. Zack Bowen and James Carens, 1984) is probably the best comprehensive statement on *Dubliners*.

Redirecting attention from the individual stories to the book as a whole and its relationship to Joyce's later works, much recent criticism of *Dubliners* focuses on questions of style, with an emphasis on the relationship between "language" and "reality," neither of which can be understood in traditional ways. Conditioned directly or indirectly

by continental literary theories—particularly structuralism and deconstruction (or poststructuralism)—such criticism frequently draws attention to subtle modulations in Joyce's rhetorical position within or
between stories (and books), emphasizing the philosophical implications of such shifts. In general, Anglo-American critics have employed
such methodologies to reinforce relatively traditional approaches to
the "meaning" or patterns of meaning in Joyce's work. Building on the
heated debate between Walzl (1965) and Robert Scholes (1964, 1967),
Bowen's "Joyce and the Epiphany Concept: A New Approach" (1981)
exemplifies the continuing insights accessible from a relatively traditional perspective. In contrast, theoretically oriented European critics—most of whom are more directly concerned with *Ulysses* and
Finnegans Wake—have challenged the entire concept of *meaning*, suggesting that the language of *Dubliners*, inevitably immersed in the paradoxes and limitations of all systems of discourse, resists and subverts
all attempts to establish a fixed reading, including those intended by
Joyce.

Critical awareness of Joyce's deepening sense of the elusiveness
and complexity of language is not entirely new. As early as 1964, Winston Weathers's prescient essay "A Portrait of the Broken Word" identified Joyce's "falling away" from the "old order of communication
into seemingly new frontiers of language and speech." Tracing Joyce's
process "from dialogue and conversation, through argument and mis-
understanding to monologue and finally to soliloquy," Weathers presented *Dubliners* as the relatively traditional point of departure on
Joyce's "downward path from a semblance of connection to a lack of
verbal contact with the world." Homer Obed Brown's excellent study
James Joyce's Early Fiction: The Biography of a Form (1972) presents
a parallel argument concerning the shifting relationship between narrator and material. Observing that the early stories in *Dubliners* posit
the existence of an external "reality" conceived as "other," Brown
notes a gradual shift toward "The Dead" in which "the narrator,
rather than standing outside, becomes a fictional role developing
within the book. Gabriel's surrender of the independence of his ego
coincides with the abandonment of the notion of a narrator indepen-

dent of the word he speaks."[13] Anticipating explicitly deconstructive readings, Brown notes that "At least part of the symbolism of *Dubliners* has to do with the failure or inadequacy of the symbol."

At about the same time Brown was publishing his crucial transitional study, several French theorists who were shortly to exert a major influence on American criticism began to turn their attention to Joyce. Although most focus on Joyce's later texts—which seemed to anticipate crucial insights of poststructuralist, post-Marxist, and/or post-Freudian theory—Hélène Cixous's "Joyce: The (r)use of Writing" (originally published 1970, English translation 1984) demonstrated the potential application of a theoretical approach to *Dubliners*. Arguing that Joyce's language casts the traditional conception of a unified character into doubt, Cixous discussed the "decentering of the subject" as revealed in the first paragraph of "The Sisters." Identifying the paragraph as "the locus of a consciousness which censorship hardly separates from the unconscious," Cixous develops concepts implied, but not fully developed, by Weathers and Brown: "representation [in *Dubliners*] is immediately modulated . . . the discourse has less bearing on a concrete outside, on a reproducable real, than on the gaze directed at the referent (the Dubliners), on the nature of that gaze, and even on the name, the letter of that gaze."[14]

During the 1970s, Joyce criticism began to develop a less provincial character as American, Irish, English, French, Swiss, and Italian critics (among others) began to establish personal and professional communications, aided in great part by the Symposia. By the publication of the anthology *Post-Structuralist Joyce: Essays from the French* (1984), English-language Joyce criticism had made large steps toward comprehending and assimilating—some would say distorting and coopting—continental theory. To some extent, this process involved a recapitulation of the internal disputes of the French theorists, which are described in accessible terms in Terry Eagleton's *Literary Theory: An Introduction* (1983). Essays such as Scholes's "Semiotic Approaches to a Fictional Text: Joyce's 'Eveline'" (1978) and the 1981 *James Joyce Quarterly* debate over the application of Seymour Chatman's *Story and Discourse* to "Araby"—which includes responses by

Chatman and Jonathan Culler—attempt to link theoretical and practical discourse on *Dubliners*. As in the 1960s when symbolic readings of individual stories proliferated, a brief glance at the titles of more recent essays on *Dubliners* reveals the developing emphasis on issues of narration, discourse, and what might be called the "significant silences" of the text. Among the more insightful of these essays are Joseph Garrison's "*Dubliners*: Portraits of the Artist as Narrator" (1975); Marilyn French's "Missing Pieces in Joyce's *Dubliners*" (1978); Mark J. Heumann's "Writing—and Not Writing—in Joyce's 'A Painful Case'" (1981); Fritz Senn's "'The Boarding House' Seen as a Tale of Misdirection" (1986); and Jean-Michel Rabaté's "Silence in *Dubliners*" (1982). Rabaté's essay, probably the least compromising poststructuralist essay on *Dubliners* to have appeared in English, concentrates on "an analysis of the exile of 'performance' in the enunciative strategies of the text, until everything will appear hinged on the silent name of the capitalized Father."[15]

While the final phrase reflects the post-Freudian emphasis of much French theoretical discourse, Rabaté's emphasis on the "discrepancy between theory and the interpretation of systems" echoes a leitmotiv linking otherwise disparate *Dubliners* criticism of the past decade. Although Colin MacCabe's attempt to synthesize political and psychological theories in *James Joyce and the Revolution of the Word* (1978) has been criticized from several perspectives, his emphasis on *Dubliners* as part of an ongoing process seems convincing. Stressing the difference between Joyce's stories and "classical realism," MacCabe concludes that they "lack any final and privileged discourse within them which dominates the others through its claim of access to the real."[16] Ultimately, this serves to heighten the reader's (implicitly political) awareness of "the imposition of our discourses on the text [and] the stereotype within our own discourses." This awareness of the relationship between the critic/reader's personal discourse and his/her reading of the text plays an indirect role in a number of more conventional readings of *Dubliners,* notably those included in C. H. Peake's *James Joyce: The Citizen and the Artist* (1977) and Bernard Benstock's *James Joyce: The Undiscover'd Country* (1977). Both

Peake, who essentially recapitulates Harry Levin's thesis of three decades earlier, and Benstock resist the urge to establish a dominant perspective for interpretation of Joyce's work. Rather, each advances a complex "neither . . . nor / both . . . and" approach to the dichotomies of engagement/separation (Peake) and Irish/continental (Benstock).

Supported by many of the theoretical essays, these books have helped shape a current consensus that *Dubliners* cannot be reduced to any single interpretation or adequately described in a single vocabulary. In this light, it seems appropriate to note that, while Joyce's later works have attracted a good deal of feminist criticism, there has been no extended attack on the sexual politics of *Dubliners*. Walzl's fine essay *"Dubliners:* Women in Irish Society" in the anthology *Women in Joyce* (1982) and Bonnie Kime Scott's *Joyce and Feminism* (1984) both conclude that *Dubliners* provides a reasonably faithful image of the actual circumstances of women's lives in turn-of-the-century Dublin.

At present, then, critical discussion of *Dubliners* seems to have reached tentative agreement that the book presents a multitude of competing discourses, none of which establishes clear dominance. This in turn reinforces a view of Joyce as a writer of *process,* rather than a creator of static masterworks. Not surprisingly, this view recurs in recent discussions of Joyce's other texts. A significant contribution to Joyce studies in general, John Paul Riquelme's *Teller and Tale in Joyce's Fiction* (1983) serves as a cogent summary of contemporary approaches to *Dubliners*. Aware of theoretical developments but employing a reasonably accessible vocabulary, Riquelme echoes MacCabe in his emphasis on *Dubliners* as part of Joyce's (by no means linear) process. Examining Joyce's stylistic revisions, Riquelme identifies "within the text an image of the author's process of discovery resembling the character's process of development."[17] Echoing Brown, Riquelme argues that this process centers on the development of a "viable style for presenting consciousness," a style in which "the recurring ambiguities of voice and presence are *not* confusions of perspective but deliberate, purposive mergings and divergings." The following statement, which reflects Riquelme's admirable ability to connect the various phases of Joyce's process without simplifying the earlier stages, both summarizes Riquelme's insights and provides a suggestive point of departure for future investigations of *Dubliners:*

> The stories of *Dubliners* are in part stylistic exercises enabling the author to explore different, though generally not wildly different, orientations toward tale and character. These exercises contribute to Joyce's developing an intimate narration of mind employing the third person rather than the first. And they allow him to practice the arrangement of narrative segments. When we look at *Dubliners* structurally as a sequence of varying but linked styles and stances of narration grouped either according to Joyce's four rubrics or according to style, the family resemblances between the collection and the three later narratives become clear. The writing of fifteen stories loosely related by overlapping elements of style furthers Joyce's eventual production of longer narratives composed of relatively discontinuous segments.[18]

Along with the pioneering work of Harry Levin and Ghiselin, the solid readings of Boyle, Walzl, and Benstock, and the stylistic inquiry of Brown, Riquelme's theoretically suggestive approach provides the critical framework for this discussion of *Dubliners.*

A R·E·A·D·I·N·G

· 4 ·

DUBLINERS AND THE
MODERNIST MILIEU

Firmly grounded in nineteenth-century realism and symbolism, *Dubliners* anticipates the modernist/postmodernist approach to art as a field of play for apparently irreconcilable perspectives. Usually—and within the usual terms, accurately—viewed as less complex than *Ulysses* and *Finnegans Wake,* Joyce's first book in some ways incorporates a wider range of possibilities than his acknowledged masterworks. Written before the stylistic devices of modernism had assumed characteristic form, *Dubliners* confronts the experience of radical dislocation that was emerging as a central aspect of Anglo-American consciousness in the decades leading up to World War I. From his position on the margins of the British Empire and Europe, Joyce both shared and remained emotionally separate from the experiences that generated the diverse responses lumped together by literary historians under the rubric of "modernism." Like most modernists texts, *Dubliners* expresses the fragmentation experienced by individuals unable to rely on old certainties, whether religious, economic, or political. Like many modernist writers, Joyce articulates this fragmentation through fragmented forms that enable him to present various perspectives while maintaining aesthetic and emotional distance. What distinguishes *Dubliners,* both historically and aesthetically, is its relative accessibility. Where the complex, formal structures and erudite allusions of many modernist texts implicitly define an audience and favor an aesthetic perspective, *Dubliners* grants equivalent attention to political, economic, and psychological, as well as aesthetic, manifestations of cultural fragmentation. Even as he began to explore the complexities that would place his later work in the modernist mainstream, the young Joyce employed a form that implies the possibility of an actual, and complex, relationship between the artist and a general audience. Repeatedly confronting the audience with images of its own paralysis, Joyce suggests the insufficiency of any single response to or analysis of this paralysis.

One of many possible approaches to *Dubliners,* literary modernism commands special attention primarily because it has provided an organizing, and at times distorting, principle for most commentary on Joyce. A term associated with a variety of movements and texts of the late nineteenth and twentieth centuries, modernism has frequently been identified with the fragmented, allusive styles of T. S. Eliot and Ezra Pound. Inasmuch as it juxtaposes its fifteen stories to create new aesthetic experiences, *Dubliners* can be related directly to this current of modernism. If accepted uncritically, however, this identification of modernism with stylistic experimentation, developed long after the publication of Joyce's book, can lead to serious distortions. Recent literary historians, taking into account previously excluded texts or aspects of texts, have come to understand modernism in terms of competing impulses—toward extremes of objectivity and subjectivity— rather than specific characteristics or techniques.

These impulses can be traced back to the origins of modernism in the gradual destruction of the medieval worldview. Grounded on the belief in an underlying structure of correspondences that ensured unity and coherence, the medieval worldview began to crumble in the face of scientific, political, economic, and philosophical challenges. Despite huge differences, Copernicus, Luther, Descartes, Napoleon, Erasmus, Darwin, Marx, and Rousseau—or to state it in terms of movements, the Reformation, romanticism, the Enlightenment, evolutionary thought, positivism, nationalism, etc.—all helped render the hierarchical worldview archaic by the late nineteenth century. The industrial revolution, accompanied by widespread urbanization and wholesale readjustments of social relationships, simply provided a focus for forces that had been transforming European culture gradually for several centuries. In addition to engendering the sense of alienation that was to develop into a popular magazine cliché by the 1920s, these transformations radically expanded the intellectual world of the early twentieth-century artist. Historical excavations in Asia and Egypt sparked a factual rather than legendary awareness of history; Freudian psychology brought new areas of human behavior under intense scrutiny; comparative anthropology began to recognize diverse cultures as internally coherent rather than simply primitive.

Responding to these forces and exploring these resources, early modernist artists pursued a multitude of individual paths. Recognizing the impossibility of an inclusive definition of modernism, literary historians have begun to understand the "movement" in terms of a dialectic between subjective and objective approaches. Suggestive rather than proscriptive, the approach to modernism as a set of interacting tensions encourages recognition of previously excluded or obscure texts and aspects of texts. Written just as the subjective and objective tendencies were assuming their characteristic forms (which would later deflect attention from other possible modernisms), *Dubliners* rewards rereading from a perspective that questions the preconceptions imposed by literary history, even though that history was based largely on Joyce's own later work.

Dubliners reflects Joyce's fascination with the objective presentation of seemingly trivial details. Every location in the book is "real." The description of North Richmond Street in "Araby" is accurate; the route walked by Corley and Lenehan in "Two Gallants" can be retraced by a contemporary visitor to Dublin. After he had moved from Dublin to Trieste, where he completed writing the stories in *Dubliners*, Joyce wrote to his brother Stanislaus to verify factual details. Among these were: the question of whether a priest could be buried in a habit, like Father Flynn in "The Sisters"; the type of police and hospital treatment that would be accorded the victim of the accident at Sydney Parade described in "A Painful Case"; and several details concerning ward boundaries and election procedures referred to in "Ivy Day in the Committee Room." During his brief residence in Rome, Joyce visited the Biblioteca Vittoria Emanuele to verify details of the Vatican Council of 1870 even though those details are comically distorted by the characters in "Grace." Combined with his use of outwardly undistinguished characters (as opposed to the "exceptional" heroes of classical literature) and his emphasis on the depressing details of the urban scene, this commitment to factual detail reflects Joyce's interest in the "scientific objectivity" of nineteenth-century realism, an interest that would receive classic expression in the immense catalogs of material objects in modernist novels such as *Ulysses* and Thomas Mann's *Buddenbrooks*.

Joyce's objective tendency extended well beyond an obsessive concern with facts. His insistence on factual accuracy and mundane detail were in part reactions against Victorian sentimentality, which he saw as a retreat to a fantasy world devoid of social and psychological tensions. In these terms, subjectivity is seen as a threat, an imposition of a limited vision that inevitably circumscribes the work of art. The semiautobiographical Stephen Dedalus in *A Portrait of the Artist as a Young Man* articulates the objective aspects of Joyce's temperament when he says: "The artist, like the God of the creation, remains within or behind or beyond or above his handiwork, invisible, refined out of existence, indifferent, paring his fingernails" (215). To a limited extent, this accurately describes the stance Joyce assumes through most of *Dubliners*. The author never enters directly into the text, never comments in his own voice. Only rarely does he directly intimate his sympathies or judgments. Like Stephen's God of the creation, or Zola's scientific novelist whose role is to insert his characters into a particular set of circumstances, the objective Joyce simply reports on what happens to Little Chandler and Jimmy Doyle, to Emily Sinico and Kathleen Kearney as they encounter a fictional Dublin as much like the real one as possible.

Reflecting only one pole of the modernist dialectic, this is, of course, only a partial description of Joyce's practice in *Dubliners*. Even

Stephen Dedalus's aesthetic of detachment resonates with unmistakable subjective undertones. Rather than denying the importance of the artist's personality, the statement radically extends it. No longer immersed in, and limited by, the environment, the Joycean artist is identified as the *source* of the environment. Objectivity is revealed as a function of a more inclusive subjectivity. From this angle, *Dubliners* can be seen not as a repudiation of, but rather as a study of the thwarting of, subjective development. The first paragraph of "The Sisters" focuses precisely on the subjective experience of the young protagonist, whose speculations on the relationship between reality and words—gnomon, simony, paralysis—mark him as a potential artist in the Joycean mode. Even those stories written in the third person usually center on a single subjective experience. The texture of James Duffy's circumscribed sensibility in "A Painful Case" commands much more interest than the details of the police response. Given the prevelance of stunted artists in *Dubliners*—Little Chandler, James Duffy, Gabriel Conroy—it is particularly easy to see the book as Joyce's intensely subjective meditation on the limitations he has overcome. Contrasting sharply with the indifference to style in many realistic novels, the self-conscious artistry of *Dubliners* may be the strongest evidence of its subjectivity. As even a cursory glance at Joyce's revisions reveals, the "objectivity reality" presented in the book, far from embodying the work of an indifferent creator, has been intricately arranged into resonant patterns of words, images, stories. No less than the symbolists immersed in the details of their own visions and dreamlives, Joyce viewed writing as an inevitable reflection of the artist's subjectivity, however extensive or veiled it might be.

Dubliners, then, can be understood as an expression of either a subjective or an objective position. The book endorses neither position; its meaning emerges from their intricate interrelationship. To the extent that Joyce valued subjectivity as such, it was not a rarified subjectivity, which would carry with it the risk of sentimentality, but an inclusive subjectivity incorporating the myriad details of everyday life. To the extent that he valued objectivity as such, it was not a circumscribed objectivity that excluded the realities of mind and feeling. Though he would later arrive at particular "Joycean" stances, *Dublin-*

ers presents his first, relatively open, articulation of the tension. As an early modernist text, *Dubliners* ironically suggests approaches that developed historically only after the overthrow of the conventional image of "high modernism" based in large part on *Ulysses*. Testing both subjective and objective approaches, *Dubliners* suggests a form of literary modernism in which the role of the artist is to confront the audience with an array of forces and perspectives as complex as that encountered in its daily experience of the world.

· 5 ·

PARALYSIS AND EPIPHANY:
THEME, STRUCTURE, STYLE

To acknowledge the multiplicity of possible approaches to *Dubliners* is not to assert the equal validity of all interpretations. Competing approaches to the book generally center on disagreements concerning the implications of what nearly all critics have recognized as Joyce's central theme: the paralysis permeating Irish life. Whatever their larger vision of modernism or Joyce's career, few take issue with Joyce's description of *Dubliners* as "a chapter in the moral history of my country . . . I chose Dublin for the scene because that city seemed to me the centre of the paralysis."[19] At times, Joyce expressed an even harsher view. As he began work on the stories, Joyce announced his intention "to betray the soul of the hemplegia or paralysis which many consider a city." Near the end of the composition process, one of his Triestine students recorded a similar remark.

> Dubliners, strictly speaking, are my fellow-countrymen, but I don't care to speak of our "dear, dirty Dublin" as they do. Dubliners are the most hopeless, useless and inconsistent race of charlatans I have ever come across. . . . The Dubliner passes his time gabbing and making the rounds in bars or taverns or cathouses, without ever getting "fed up" with the double doses of whiskey and Home Rule,

and at night, when he can hold no more and is swollen up with poison like a toad, he staggers from the side-door and, guided by an instinctive desire for stability along the straight line of the houses, he goes slithering his backside against all walls and corners. He goes "arsing along" as we say in English. There's the Dubliner for you.[20]

After he had finished the book, Joyce occasionally tempered his judgment. In a 1906 letter to his brother Stanislaus, he admitted that "Sometimes thinking of Ireland it seems to me that I have been unnecessarily harsh. I have reproduced (in *Dubliners* at least) none of the attraction of the city for I have never felt at my ease in any city since I left it except in Paris. I have not reproduced its ingenuous insularity and its hospitality. The latter 'virtue' so far as I can see does not exist elsewhere in Europe. I have not been just to its beauty."[21] Far from mitigating the severity of Joyce's criticism, such retrospective self-questioning attests to its power. Portraying both literal and figurative paralysis, *Dubliners* delineates its origins in and impact on Irish religious, political, economic, and familial institutions. In a book built around carefully repeated and varied image patterns, many of the most haunting images—the harpist in "Two Gallants," the darkened bazaar in "Araby"—draw their power from the connection between seemingly distinct dimensions of the paralysis.

PARALYSIS AS THEME

Reinforced by numerous structural patterns, the theme of paralysis is firmly established almost immediately. The first paragraph of "The Sisters," the first story in the book, begins: "There was no hope for him this time: it was the third stroke." It concludes: "Every night as I gazed up at the window I said softly to myself the word *paralysis*. It has always sounded strangely in my ears, like the word *gnomon* in the Euclid and the word *simony* in the Catechism. But now it sounded to me like the name of some maleficent and sinful being. It filled me with fear, and yet I longed to be nearer to it and to look upon its deadly work." The remainder of *Dubliners* fulfills this longing. A comparison of the version of "The Sisters" published in the *Irish Homestead* (13 August 1904) with the revised version reveals that the explicit emphasis on paralysis was a late addition. The early version reads:

> Three nights in succession I had found myself in Great Britain Street at that hour, as if by Providence. Three nights also I had raised my eyes to that lighted square of window and speculated. I seemed to understand that it would occur at night. But in spite of the Providence that had led my feet, and in spite of the reverent curiosity of my eyes, I had discovered nothing. Each night the square was lighted in some way, faintly and evenly. It was not the light of candles so far as I could see. Therefore it had not yet occurred.

The physical circumstance remains the same in each version; the young boy awaits the death of the priest who has befriended him. As L. J. Morrissey notes in his essay on "Joyce's Revision of 'The Sisters': From Epicleti to Modern Fiction" (1986), the metaphorical resonance of the revised version differs sharply from the original. Where the first version is unremittingly abstract—the object of the boy's speculation remains unstated—the second version specifies the illness (the strokes) before elevating it to a metaphysical level. The stroke manifests the general paralysis that provides a center for the boy's speculations. The undefined words *gnomon*—an incomplete geometrical figure—and *simony*—the sin of buying or selling spiritual entities—introduce additional dimensions of the paralysis portrayed in *Dubliners*.

If the theme of paralysis was not explicit in the first version of "The Sisters," it emerged very early in Joyce's work on the volume as a whole. The second and third of Joyce's stories to be published in the *Irish Homestead* present distinct, if relatively uncomplicated, varieties of paralysis. Published 10 September 1904, "Eveline" focuses on the literal paralysis of the title character. Offered an alternative to life with her abusive father, Eveline Hill ponders moving to Buenos Aires with her lover, Frank. The opening paragraph emphasizes her immobility: "She sat at the window watching the evening invade the avenue. Her head was leaned against the window curtains and in her nostrils was the odour of dusty cretonne. She was tired." Even the verb form— "her head *was* leaned"—testifies to Eveline's passivity. Although her deadening life in Dublin engenders sudden surges of terror that urge her to "Escape! She must escape!," she fails to overcome her immobility. The final section of the story focuses on Eveline's decision whether or not to go with Frank. Underlining her paralysis, Joyce provides no image of her movement from home to station. Rather, she is pictured as passive, a static figure "among the swaying crowd in the station." She is capable only of "moving her lips in silent fervent prayer." As a result, her urge to escape collapses. As Frank calls to her, "She set her white face to him, passive, like a helpless animal. Her eyes gave him no sign of love or farewell or recognition." Like Bob Doran and Polly Mooney in "The Boarding House" or James Duffy and Emily Sinico in "A Painful Case," Eveline cannot conceive of a real alternative to her present circumstances; the resulting failure of courage enforces her paralysis.

If many cases of paralysis in *Dubliners* are literal, rendering the characters incapable of movement, Joyce was aware that motion per se provided no real alternative. The third Joyce story published in the *Irish Homestead* (17 December 1904), "After the Race," opens with an image of motion: "The cars came scudding in towards Dublin, running evenly like pellets in the groove of the Naas Road." Already, however, the imagery identifies the motion as purely mechanical. As "pellets in the groove," the cars—and their riders—have very little freedom of movement. The second sentence describes Ireland as a "channel of poverty and inaction," contrasting with the superficial glamour of the continental race cars. Joyce brings the theme into focus through his portrayal of Jimmy Doyle, the young Irishman accompanying the French drivers and their Hungarian companion in one of the cars. Despite his English education, Jimmy feels trapped by his Irish heritage and seeks desperately for an escape: "Rapid motion through space elates one; so does notoriety; so does the possession of money. These were three good reasons for Jimmy's excitement." Providing no lasting escape, physical or emotional, this sense of exhilaration serves only to further Jimmy's entrapment. By the end of the card game that takes place in a closed cabin aboard a yacht, Jimmy has lost a substantial amount of money. His escape has been little more than an illusion propagated by his ostensible friends in order to ensure his further victimization. The final image of the Hungarian opening the cabin door simply emphasizes that Jimmy has fallen back into an enclosure without even realizing it. As Florence Walzl notes, although Joyce never fully revised "After the Race," he did add the phrase "glad of the dark stupor that would cover up his folly" to the closing paragraph, suggesting the underlying similarity of Eveline and Jimmy. As with the literal image of paralysis, the image of "motion as paralysis" recurs frequently in *Dubliners*. The quests of the boys in "Araby" and "An Encounter," the wandering of Corley and Lenehan in "Two Gallants," and the train trip of Maria in "Clay" all involve physical motion. In no case, however, does aimless movement help any character escape the encompassing paralysis.

The passive and active forms of paralysis coalesce in the impact of Irish institutions on individuals. Eveline and Jimmy Doyle differ only in superficial details. Neither has any sense of a life not dictated by external forces. Despite their differences concerning his aesthetic stance, critics have agreed that Joyce strongly criticizes Irish religion, politics, economics, and family life. In "Eveline," he emphasizes the role of religion in enforcing paralysis. Joyce's description of the Hill household includes "the coloured print of the promises made to Blessed Margaret Mary Alacoque," whose vision of Christ's heart lead to the founding of the Order of the Sacred Heart. A common emblem of devotion in Irish Catholic households, the print promises domestic peace to the faithful, a particularly ironic promise in light of the brutality of Eveline's father. Nonetheless, Catholicism maintains a firm hold over Eveline's actions. As she stands at the station, the only action she can conceive of is prayer: "she prayed to God to direct her"; "she kept moving her lips in silent fervent prayer." Clearly, Eveline's reliance on religion for guidance contributes to her passivity. From the dead priest in "The Sisters" through Father Purdon in "Grace"—

whose view of the Lord as a kind of chief accountant reiterates the theme of simony from the first paragraph—the Catholic Church fares poorly throughout *Dubliners*. Joyce portrays the clergy as at best ineffectual, at worst actively malevolent.

Nor do political institutions escape blame for the Irish paralysis. Less explicit than "Ivy Day in the Committee Room," "After the Race" addresses the political problem in its description of Jimmy's father. Although he "had begun life as an advanced Nationalist," Jimmy's father reenacts the pattern of betrayal that Joyce saw as the defining element of Irish politics. Distancing himself from the Home Rule movement—he "had modified his views early"—Mr. Doyle establishes himself as a successful butcher. Eventually, he is able to "secure some of the police contracts" and grows "rich enough to be alluded to in the Dublin newspapers as a merchant prince." This form of success requires that Mr. Doyle abandon political commitment. Moreover, he perpetuates the Irish sense of inferiority by sending his son to school in England, where he can "see a little life." Such actions guarantee that Ireland will remain a "channel of poverty and inaction." Only half-conscious that he is very much affected by the general malaise, Jimmy finds that his education provides no effective response. The economic dependence of the Irish upon the English, which discourages political activity, echoes throughout *Dubliners*. Joyce's emphasis on the English accents of the young men bantering with the salesgirl in "Araby" and on the "North of Ireland accent" of Farrington's supervisor in "Counterparts" reiterates the underlying connection between the political and economic forces circumscribing Dublin life.

These institutional pressures severely distort Irish family life. As the patterns in both "Eveline" and "After the Race" suggest, the most immediate sources of paralysis lie in the family. Each subsequent generation re-creates its own victimization. Although Eveline's mother has lived a "life of common-place sacrifices closing in final craziness," she makes her daughter "promise to keep the home together as long as she could." By sending Jimmy to Cambridge, Mr. Doyle locks his son into the mentality that forced him to repudiate his own nationalism. Despite her own unhappy marriage, Mrs. Mooney in "The Boarding House" fights to obtain a husband for her daughter; perpetuating her own frustration, Mrs. Kearney in "A Mother" effectively undercuts Kathleen's musical career; humiliated by his boss in "Counterparts," Farrington terrorizes his son. At no point does Joyce indicate that any Irish institution—religious, political, economic, familial—can or will play a significant role in helping individuals cope with the overwhelming sense of social and psychological paralysis.

STRUCTURAL PATTERNS

By the time he finished "The Sisters," "Eveline," and "After the Race," Joyce had identified paralysis as the central theme of *Dubliners*. As he continued work on the individual stories, he began to conceive of them as a unified book. As early as July 1904, he wrote to Constance Curran (one of the models for Gabriel Conroy in "The Dead"): "I am writing a series of epicleti—ten—for a paper. I have written one. I call the series *Dubliners*."[22] The term *epicleti* derives from the Greek term *epicleseis*, an element of the eastern Orthodox mass in which the Holy Ghost is invoked to transform the host into the blood and body of Christ. In addition to anticipating the concept of the epiphany, Joyce's comment makes it clear that he was seeking a form that would enable the individual stories to echo and comment on one another, thereby expanding the significance of apparently trivial events.

By 24 September 1905, the plan had assumed much clearer shape. Joyce had been working rapidly, drafting eight stories between April and October. As he began thinking of a second book of short stories to be titled *Provincials*, Joyce announced the plan of *Dubliners* in a letter to Stanislaus: "The order of the stories is as follows. *The Sisters, An Encounter* and another story which are stories of my childhood: *The Boarding House, After the Race* and *Eveline*, which are stories of adolescence: *The Clay, Counterparts*, and *A Painful Case* which are stories of mature life: *Ivy Day in the Committee Room, A Mother* and the last story of the book which are stories of public life in Dublin."[23] Although Joyce would eventually add three more stories (in addition to "Araby" and "Grace," the two as yet unwritten stories mentioned in the letter), this structural plan would remain essentially intact.

"Two Gallants" joins the stories of adolescence; "A Little Cloud" the stories of maturity. Usually filed with the stories of public life for convenience, "The Dead"—written more than a year after any of the other stories—serves as a coda that summarizes and extends Joyce's major concerns.

Framed by two stories focusing on physically or spiritually paralyzed priests ("The Sisters," "Grace"), the early version of *Dubliners* is characterized by a classical balance and symmetry. The intense individualism of the first three stories—the only stories written in the first person—contrasts with the relative lack of emphasis on individuals in the final three stories. The young adults of the second section—Joyce employed the classical definition of adolescence as extending through the twenties—prefigure the isolated middle-aged characters of the third section. Each triad of stories has a distinctive image structure, relating to its particular relationship to the theme of paralysis. The first triad includes numerous images of attempted escape; the second of traps; the third of isolation; the fourth of public buildings. Each of the last three triads juxtaposes men and women at similar stages of their lives. Any two triads can be juxtaposed with one another to reveal the interrelationship of particular aspects of paralysis. "Eveline" and "Clay" share a concern with the situation of the unmarried woman; "The Boarding House" and "Counterparts" trace the male relationship to marriage; "Araby" and "A Painful Case" consider the significance of isolation and feelings of superiority at different stages of life. The list of resonances within and between triads can be extended indefinitely.

The addition of "Two Gallants" and "A Little Cloud" did little to alter the underlying currents of the original triads. It did, however, mark an important loosening of the classical architecture of the original plan. In effect, Joyce adjusts his formal structure to incorporate new material, rather than forcing the material into a preconceived structure. This suggests a second pattern operating in *Dubliners*, one reflected in the sequence of composition, rather than the final structure of the book. The first stories Joyce wrote—"The Sisters," "Eveline," and "After the Race"—are relatively simple statements of the paralysis theme. As he continued to write, Joyce developed distinct approaches to the theme during particular periods, later incorporating these approaches into the four-part structure. Between April and July of 1905, for example, Joyce wrote "A Painful Case," "The Boarding House," and "Counterparts," three of his most savage stories. The latter two, both finished in mid-July, share a naturalistic concern with the environment as trap and with physical and emotional brutality. "Grace" and "Araby," the last two stories mentioned in Joyce's original plan, are the most overtly mythological sections of *Dubliners*. The two later additions, "A Little Cloud" and "Two Gallants," anticipate the complex psychological techniques that would be put to extended use in "The Dead." The addition of "The Dead" to the expanded book that Grant Richards accepted for publication both enriched the existing patterns and created new structures. Perhaps the most significant pattern to emerge from the addition involves the framework of opening story ("The Sisters"), closing story ("The Dead"), and central story ("A Little Cloud"). The elderly sisters and public ritual of "The Dead" balance "The Sisters" as nicely as would the paralyzed priest of "Grace." Slowly surrendering his active impulses and settling into a paralysis he is still capable of experiencing as torment, Little Chandler in "A Little Cloud" links the young narrator of the opening story with Gabriel Conroy in "The Dead." Recognizing such patterns as outgrowths of Joyce's process of composition does not negate the significance of the original plan; rather, it suggests that patterns of images and themes permeate the volume on several different levels.

Each of the four sections of *Dubliners* develops a particular aspect of the theme of paralysis. The stories of childhood—"The Sisters," "An Encounter," and "Araby"—picture early confrontations of young boys (or perhaps a single young boy) with their corrupt environment. Although each is still capable of desiring and conceiving some form of escape—whether the internal meditations of "The Sisters," the actual journey of "An Encounter," or the psychological quest of "Araby"—all experience deep disillusionment. In effect, Joyce suggests that the external environment crushes the individual sensibility, encouraging even the more sensitive Irish children to accept and internalize paralysis. The stories of adolescence explore the characters' inability to challenge that paralysis. The male protagonists of "After the

Race" and "Two Gallants" attempt to substitute motion and intrigue for actual confrontation with the sources of corruption. For the women in "Eveline" and "The Boarding House," paralysis assumes a more literal form, leading them to accept, at times to desire, their own victimization.

Casting the term "maturity" in an ironic light, the third sequence of stories demonstrates the long-range implications of the choices made, or not made, during adolescence. Although they hide the knowledge from themselves, the protagonists of "A Little Cloud," "Counterparts," "Clay," and "A Painful Case" have surrendered utterly to paralysis. Their longing for escape emerges only momentarily and is repressed whenever real action seems possible. Following this blistering critique of Irish "maturity," Joyce brings several groups of mature Dubliners together in the stories of public life. Focusing on political ("Ivy Day in the Committee Room"), cultural ("A Mother"), and religious ("Grace") life, Joyce demonstrates the interaction between institutions. The poem in "Ivy Day in the Committee Room" reflects Dublin cultural life; the concert in "A Mother" is political in origin. The presence of relatively young characters in "Ivy Day in the Committee Room" and "A Mother" reiterates the themes of the opening triad. "The Dead," which will be discussed in detail below, extends the themes of the stories of public life: the absence of a public language capable of articulating deep feeling; the evasion of underlying tensions; the absence of real communication between men and women. But the qualitatively different treatment of Gabriel's consciousness, made possible by Joyce's stylistic maturation, justifies viewing the final story as a new structural element, a coda that significantly revises the vision of paralysis expressed in the original plan.

"SCRUPULOUS MEANNESS" AND THE PARALYSIS OF LANGUAGE

Throughout his career, Joyce was obsessed with language. In part, this obsession reflects his belief that the impoverishment of language both in ordinary conversation and formal public discourse played a crucial role in the paralysis described in *Dubliners*. The absence of a vital language infects the characters' thought process, rendering them progressively less capable of communicating any important truth. Joyce attempted to resolve the problem by combining a relatively sparse writing style with the concept of the "epiphany" to articulate perceptions inherent, but not capable of being expressed, within the paralyzed context. Frequently used as the touchstone for discussion of Joyce's style from his early notebooks through his mature novels, the term *epiphany* has no static meaning. Rather, Joyce uses the epiphany as a way of engaging the ongoing process of adjustment between language and perception. Exploring the connection between various stages of such processes, most notably in "The Dead," Joyce develops a style capable of mediating the epiphanies of character, narrator/author, and reader.

In a letter to Grant Richards, Joyce described the style of *Dubliners* as "a style of scrupulous meanness," adding that "he is a very bold man who dares to alter in the presentment, still more to deform, whatever he has seen and heard."[24] By no means adequate to the range of styles employed in *Dubliners,* this description nonetheless identifies the base for Joyce's later embellishments. Focusing on external details and employing a minimal amount of ornamentation, Joyce creates a distance between his own voice and those of his characters, limited to the paralyzed and paralyzing language of their environment. Written in direct sentences and employing a vocabulary accessible to readers of newspaper prose, the following passage from "Two Gallants" typifies Joyce's "scrupulously mean" style:

> He turned to the left when he came to the corner of Rutland Square and felt more at ease in the dark quiet street, the sombre look of which suited his mood. He paused at last before the window of a poor-looking shop over which the words *Refreshment Bar* were printed in white letters. On the glass of the window were two flying inscriptions: *Ginger Beer* and *Ginger Ale*. A cut ham was exposed on a great blue dish while near it on a plate lay a segment of very light plum-pudding. He eyed this food earnestly for some time and then, after glancing warily up and down the street, went into the shop quickly.

Realistic in approach, this stripped down writing presents the reader with a clear visual image. Joyce's stance in such passages resembles that of the ideal newspaper reporter who simply transmits facts without editorial comment.

The strategic purpose of this scrupulously mean style relates to Joyce's belief that unembellished facts would communicate his central theme of paralysis. Nowhere is this clearer than in his explicit treatment of language as theme. In *Dubliners*, all modes of communication—direct speech, formal discourse, even the early forms of stream of consciousness—are severely impoverished. Only rarely does Joyce present actual conversation at any length. Although "A Painful Case" centers on the intellectual relationship between James Duffy and Emily Sinico, only Emily's first line—"What a pity there is such a poor house to-night! It's so hard on people to have to sing to empty benches"—is reported in the form of direct speech. With the exception of a few lines quoted in the newspaper clipping, the rest of the story is a third-person limited presentation of Duffy's response. In "Clay" only a few trivial lines of conversation are presented as speech; the rest of the story is mediated through Maria's consciousness. Implicitly commenting on the absence of real communication in spoken language, Joyce transforms conversation into internal monologue, emphasizing his characters' self-absorption. Joyce's description of the old man's monologue in "An Encounter" provides an emblem for the underlying dynamic of most speech in *Dubliners*: "His mind, as if magnetised again by his speech, seemed to circle slowly round and round its new centre." Even when Joyce includes actual conversation, language distorts, veils, or evades communication as in the following passage from "The Sisters":

     —Did he . . . peacefully? she asked.

     —O, quite peacefully, ma'am, said Eliza. You couldn't tell when the breath went out of him. He had a beautiful death, God be praised.

     —And everything . . .?

     —Father O'Rourke was in with him a Tuesday and anointed him and prepared him and all.

Both the gaps in questions and the reassuring answers, which are negated by the facts of Father Flynn's death that emerge later in the story, underscore the evasiveness of the language that surrounds the young narrator.

Similarly, public speech in *Dubliners*—with the possible exception of Gabriel's dinner speech in "The Dead"—provides no language capable of resisting paralysis. However heartfelt the emotion, Hynes's poem "The Death of Parnell" in "Ivy Day in the Committee Room" collapses under the weight of clichés and self-consciously poetic language. The political and emotional dimensions of "A Mother" recede behind the petty bickering over contractual detail. Even more extreme, the sermon that concludes "Grace" (originally intended as the final story in *Dubliners*) testifies primarily to the prevalence of a language unable to distinguish spiritual from economic truths: "Well, I have looked into my accounts. I find this wrong and this wrong. But, with God's grace, I will rectify this and this. I will set right my accounts."

Given this debased public language, the impoverishment of internal speech seems inevitable. Only the stories of childhood—and again, perhaps, "The Dead"—intimate any possibility of a different sense of language. Where Father Purdon's sermon has no name for sin—it is referred to only indirectly as "this and this"—the narrator of "The Sisters" associates evil precisely with the phenomenon of language dissociated from meaning. Contemplating the word *paralysis,* the boy attributes to it an active presence that he wishes to observe rather than evade: "now it sounded to me like the name of some maleficent and sinful being. It filled me with fear, and yet I longed to be nearer to it and to look upon its deadly work." However intense this desire, it receives no support from the boy's environment. Joyce implies that, by the time he matures, the boy will be reduced to the more profound silence of the adult characters, most of whom are no longer aware of the gap between language and experience.

This concern with the relationship between language and experience presented Joyce with the problem of how to communicate the gradual incursion of linguistic paralysis without compromising his scrupulously mean style. His solution was to link the style of each story to the consciousness of an individual, or on occasion individuals. Labeled the "Uncle Charles Principle" by Hugh Kenner (and, in slightly different terms, applied brilliantly to *Dubliners* by John Paul Riquelme), this approach enabled Joyce to develop a sequence of appropriate styles, each implying a somewhat different, but always implicit and indeterminate, relationship between author and character. The most obvious example of Joyce's thematically significant style is the shift from first to third person narration after "Araby," a shift predicated on the gradual diminishing of individual vitality. In essence, the "Uncle Charles Principle" states that word choices, syntax, idioms, etc., should be understood as expressions of, and implicit commentary on, the most important character in the textual passage in question. A comparison of passages concerned with similar material illustrates the significance of this characteristic Joycean device. The self-consciously formal, if somewhat simple, vocabulary of the following passage from "Clay" combines with the absence of well-defined conjunctions to create a powerful image of Maria's paralysis, which is at once linguistic and social: "But Joe said it didn't matter and made her sit down by the fire. He was very nice with her. He told her all that went on in his office, repeating for her a smart answer which he had made to the manager. Maria did not understand why Joe laughed so much over the answer he had made but she said that the manager must have been a very overbearing person to deal with." In contrast, the description of the "smart answer" to the manager in "Counterparts" implies a very different, if no less impoverished, sense of communication:

> Nosey Flynn was sitting up in his usual corner of Davy Byrne's and, when he heard the story, he stood Farrington a half-one, saying it was as smart a thing as ever he heard. Farrington stood a drink in his turn. After a while O'Halloran and Paddy Leonard came in and the story was repeated to them. O'Halloran stood tailors of malt, hot, all round and told the story of the retort he had made to the chief clerk when he was in Callan's of Fownes's Street; but, as the retort was after the manner of the liberal shepherds in the eclogues, he had to admit that it was not so clever as Farrington's retort. At this Farrington told the boys to polish off that and have another.

In each case, the story emphasizes the characters' refusal to confront the tensions of their lives. What differentiates them is Joyce's style. The simplicity of the first passage, reflecting Maria's willingness to accept the condescension of her relatives, gives way to the rambling, almost circular, style of the pub talk, which distracts Farrington and his friends from the powerlessness that drives them to excessive drink. Throughout *Dubliners,* Joyce's stylistic choices balance objective precision and psychological appropriateness.

Gradually, the two concerns merge as Joyce begins to emphasize the interdependence of psychology and reality, an interdependence mediated, if not determined, by an impoverished language. Ultimately, he perceives the problems faced by the characters portrayed in *Dubliners* as analogous to those he faced in writing the book. Moving gradually away from the "journalistic" objectivity of the early stories, he eventually developed more subtle techniques that allowed him to express more complex forms of irony. In the early stories, he frequently assumes a judgmental pose expressed in the fairly obvious irony of "After the Race" or "Eveline." By the time he wrote the final stories, particularly "A Little Cloud" and "The Dead," Joyce had developed a voice that allows the irony to flow both from author to character and from character back to author.

VARIETIES OF THE EPIPHANY

Joyce's shift from the straightforward "scrupulousness" of the early stories to the more complex psychological style of "The Dead" was accompanied by a parallel change in his approach to the epiphany. Although the changes have lead some critics to dispute the relevance of the term to *Dubliners,* few dispute that the book reflects Joyce's continuing concern with the way in which seemingly insignificant details could reveal complex truths. Moving away from his original view of the epiphany as a revelation of transcendent spiritual truth, Joyce gradually focuses his attention on the experience of the revelation. Juxtaposing an aesthetic of essence with an aesthetic of process, *Dub-*

liners is as much a meditation on the nature of epiphany as a compendium of epiphanies expressing particular truths.

The controversy over the application of the term epiphany results from its history in Joyce's writing. Derived from the Catholic liturgy, *epiphany* is defined theologically as "a visible manifestation of a hidden divinity in the form of a personal appearance, or by some deed of power by which its presence is made known." Aware of this concept from his Catholic education, Joyce transformed the epiphany into an aesthetic concept in *Stephen Hero,* the abandoned version of *A Portrait of the Artist as a Young Man.* There, Stephen Daedalus suddenly perceives the inner significance of a trivial snatch of conversation between a young man and young woman. The following passage from *Stephen Hero* provides Joyce's basic definition of the epiphany: "This triviality made him think of collecting many such moments together in a book of epiphanies. By an epiphany he meant a sudden spiritual manifestation whether in the vulgarity of speech or of gesture or in a memorable phase of the mind itself. He believed that it was for the man of letters to record these epiphanies with extreme care, seeing that they themselves are the most delicate and evanescent of moments." Drawing on Aquinus's aesthetic principles of unity, harmony, and radiance, Stephen concludes his speculation: "This is the moment which I call epiphany. First we recognize that the object is *one* integral thing, then we recognize that it is an organized composite structure, a *thing* in fact: finally, when the relation of the parts is exquisite, when the parts are adjusted to the special point, we recognize that it is *that* thing which it is. Its soul, its whatness, leaps to us from the vestment of its appearance. The soul of the commonest object, the structure of which is so adjusted, seems to us radiant. The object achieves its epiphany."

These passages contain several ambiguities. First, the inspiration for an epiphany may be mundane ("the vulgarity of speech or of gesture") or rarified ("a memorable phase of the mind itself"). Second, the epiphany may be inherent in the material ("its soul, its whatness, leaps to us") or created, presumably by the artist ("the structure of which is so adjusted"). Joyce seems to have been aware of these tensions from his earliest experiments with the epiphany form, a sequence of some seventy short prose sketches written between 1900 and 1903. Robert Scholes and Richard Kain, who first published the surviving sketches in their sourcebook *The Workshop of Daedalus*, identify two types of epiphanies, distinctive in content and form. Associated with rarified material and the shaping presence of the artist, the "lyrical" epiphanies describe vivid, dreamlike states. Frequently, as in epiphany number 30 from the Scholes-Kain collection, the lyrical epiphanies celebrate the spirit of the artist as it breaks away from the constraints of its environment: "The spell of arms and voices—the white arms of roads, their promise of close embraces and the black arms of tall ships that stand against the moon, their tale of distant nations. They are held out to say: We are alone,—come. And the voices say with them: We are your people. And the air is thick with their company as they call me their kinsman, making ready to go, shaking the wings of their exultant and terrible youth." Contrasting sharply with such exuberance, most "dramatic epiphanies" reveal the paralysis of the environment. Frequently they are presented in the form of dramatic scenes with stage directions. Epiphany number 10, which suggests the paralyzing conspiracy of Irish religion and art, typifies the "dramatic" form:

> [Dublin: in the Stag's Head
> Dame Lane]
> O'Mahony—Haven't you that little priest that
>   writes poetry over there—Fr Russell?
> Joyce—O, yes . . . I hear he has written verses.
> O'Mahony—*(smiling adroitly)* . . . Verses, yes . . . that's
>   the proper name for them. . . .

None of the epiphanies from Joyce's notebooks appears in *Dubliners*, a fact that has lead Scholes to argue that the term should not be applied to Joyce's stories. Nonetheless, a brief glance at Joyce's use of the epiphanies in *Stephen Hero* and *A Portrait of the Artist as a Young Man*, combined with his statements concerning the technique of *Dubliners*, demonstrates a consistent concern with the relationship between ephemeral detail and inner significance. One recurring concern involves the nature of the "spiritual manifestation" referred to in both the liturgical tradition and the definition of the epiphany included in *Stephen Hero*. Joyce's notebooks include no commentary on or context for the epiphanies. Each appears to express a self-sufficient truth equally valid for all observers struck by its Thomastic radiance. The first extended use of the epiphanies in *Stephen Hero* reinforces this general approach. Like Stephen Daedalus, Joyce takes the truth revealed by the epiphanies quite seriously; for the young artist, the memorable phases of the mind (the lyrical epiphanies) testify to a spiritual capability that distances him from the paralysis manifested in the dramatic epiphanies. By the time he wrote *A Portrait of the Artist as a Young Man*, however, Joyce's perspective had altered substantially. Each section of *Portrait* ends with an epiphany, though not all were drawn from the notebooks. Unlike the earlier versions, however, these epiphanies are subject to ironic deflation. Chapter 1, for example, climaxes with a lyrical epiphany expressing Stephen's triumph over the unjust punishment of his teachers. Immediately grounding the exhilaration in the realities of Stephen's life, chapter 2 begins with the image of Stephen's Uncle Charles exiled to the outhouse because of the foul smell of his tobacco. Although the first section of chapter 2 concludes with another of Stephen's lyrical epiphanies, the second section concludes with Simon Dedalus retelling the "triumph" as a comic story illustrating Stephen's delusion. Revoiced in dramatic terms, the lyrical epiphany stands revealed as a transitory moment in an ongoing process of revelation and reevaluation.

Written prior to the transformation of *Stephen Hero* into *A Portrait of the Artist as a Young Man*, *Dubliners* marks a transitional stage in Joyce's understanding of the epiphany. Although he had not yet adopted the ironic vision of *Portrait*, Joyce had clearly begun to understand the contingent quality of the epiphany: the fact that no revelation exists entirely apart from the perceiving consciousness. Although he did not use the term *epiphany* directly in relation to his stories, Joyce's description of the technique in *Dubliners* emphasizes precisely the transition from essence to process. Employing a term derived from the invocation in which the Holy Ghost is asked to transform the host into the blood and body of Christ, Joyce referred to his stories as "a series of epicleti." Reflecting his growing awareness of the complications inherent in his original concept of the epiphany, the new term shifts emphasis from the manifestation of the object itself to the process of transformation. Joyce's comments to his brother Stanislaus from the same period reflect his sense of himself as artistic trans-former: "Don't you think there is a certain resemblance between the mystery of the Mass and what I am trying to do? I mean that I am trying . . . to give people some intellectual pleasure or spiritual enjoyment by converting the bread of everyday life into something that has a permanent artistic life of its own."[25] The emphasis on the artist as priestlike figure connects this statement with the elevation of the lyrical epiphanies in *Stephen Hero,* which dates from the same period. The transformation of mundane details, which lies at the core of the epiphany and was to fascinate Joyce throughout his life, was very much in his mind as he wrote *Dubliners.* Anticipating the events of "A Painful Case," Joyce told Stanislaus: "Do you see that man who has just skipped out of the way of the tram? Consider, if he had been run over, how significant every act of his would at once become. I don't mean for the police inspector. I mean for anybody who knew him. And his thoughts, for anybody that could know them. It is my idea of the significance of trivial things that I want to give the two or three unfortunate wretches who may eventually read me."[26] Preparing for the intricate formal experiments in the later stories written for *Dubliners,* this statement suggests that all epiphanies are contingent on context (the events that frame the mundane gesture) and on the perceptions of the observer (*"my idea* of the significance").

Applied to individual stories in *Dubliners,* these backgrounds raise three main questions. First, precisely where is the epiphany to be found? Second, who experiences the epiphany—character, reader, and/or authorial observer? Third, what truth does the epiphany manifest? While the answers to each question are complex, several observations seem generally applicable. As Joyce's substitution of *epicleti* for *epiphany* suggests, the epiphanies in *Dubliners* seem far less localized than those in the notebooks. With the exception of several early stories, it is possible to argue cogently for at least two—and sometimes as many as a dozen—epiphanies in each story. On occasion, different characters experience epiphanies at different points. The epiphany perceived by narrator or reader may result from the juxtaposition of various characters' epiphanies. As Joyce increases his stylistic control, subtle distinctions between the perspectives of narrator and character begin to take on greater importance. Even when a particular passage is accepted as an epiphany, it may support radically differing meanings. What seems a lyrical epiphany to a character, may be a dramatic epiphany for narrator or reader.

An examination of several epiphanies, or possible epiphanies, illustrates the range of Joyce's practice and the difficulty this poses for determining the meaning of a particular epiphany. Written in a narrative voice distanced from the perspective of any character, the final section of "Counterparts" closely resembles the dramatic epiphanies from the notebooks. It concludes with a naturalistic picture of the violence directed at Farrington's son:

> The boy uttered a squeal of pain as the stick cut his thigh. He clasped his hands together in the air and his voice shook with fright.
> —O, pa! he cried. Don't beat me, pa! And I'll . . . I'll say a *Hail Mary* for you. . . . I'll say a *Hail Mary* for you, pa, if you don't beat me. . . . I'll say a *Hail Mary*. . . .

Considered on its own, this epiphany reveals the violence at the core of Irish society and suggests that religion offers little save an ineffectual illusion of protection. Introduced by a scrupulously mean passage that diminishes any possible sympathy for the boy's parents—"His wife was a little sharp-faced woman who bullied her husband when he was sober and was bullied by him when he was drunk"—the epiphany is experienced by narrator and readers, rather than the morally paralyzed characters.

The situation is somewhat more complex in the extended epiphany that concludes "A Painful Case." Considered out of context, James Duffy's vision of his own isolation resembles the lyrical epiphanies of Stephen Daedalus. Standing atop Magazine Hill, Duffy experiences a moment in which a seemingly trivial detail blossoms forth in what he feels as a spiritual truth:

> Beyond the river he saw a goods train winding out of Kingsbridge Station, like a worm with a fiery head winding through the darkness, obstinately and laboriously. It passed slowly out of sight; but still he heard in his ears the laborious drone of the engine reiterating the syllables of her name.
>
> He turned back the way he had come, the rhythm of the engine pounding in his ears. He began to doubt the reality of what memory told him. He halted under a tree and allowed the rhythm to die away. He could not feel her near him in the darkness nor her voice touch his ear. He waited for some minutes listening. He could hear nothing: the night was perfectly silent. He listened again: perfectly silent. He felt that he was alone.

Unlike Farrington in "Counterparts," Duffy experiences this scene as an epiphany. Transformed into a symbolically resonant "worm with a fiery head," the train manifests Duffy's uneasy conscience, condemning his self-imposed isolation. From a wider perspective, however, the epiphany suggests additional meanings. As the sentence "He began to doubt the reality of what memory told him" intimates, there are serious gaps in Duffy's understanding. Ironically, in the very act of accepting his culpability for Emily Sinico's death, Duffy evades and perpetuates the cause of his guilt: the profound solipsism that renders him incapable of accepting the validity of any experience other than his own. As he had done throughout his entirely platonic relationship with Mrs. Sinico, Duffy perceives only his own needs. No evidence from any other source supports his belief that Mrs. Sinico committed suicide, or was driven to despair, by his actions. A comprehensive understanding of the epiphany that concludes "A Painful Case" must take into account both the accuracy and the limitation of Duffy's view.

Descrepancies between various experiences of a particular epiphany do not always dictate harsher judgment of the character. Although it is narrated in the first person, "Araby," like "A Painful

Case," concludes with a passage that is likely to be understood differently by character and reader. Disappointed by the collapse of his romantic quest, the boy experiences a lyrical epiphany that reveals his own inadequacy: "Gazing up into the darkness I saw myself as a creature driven and derided by vanity; and my eyes burned with anguish and anger." From an external perspective, however, this self-condemnation seems overly harsh. Rather than revealing the boy's inadequacy, the epiphany can be seen as a dramatic manifestation of the process through which an otherwise healthy personality internalizes paralysis. Or, it can be understood as the first stage in the development of a destructive solipsism similar to Duffy's. However it is understood, the meaning of the epiphany depends on the interpretive perspective. In addition, it should be noted that the final paragraph is only one of several possible epiphanies in "Araby." Like the clanking of the coins on the salver, the conversation between the salesgirl and the two men with English accents recalls the dramatic epiphanies from the notebook.

—O, I never said such a thing!
—O, but you did!
—O, but I didn't!
—Didn't she say that?
—Yes. I heard her.
—O, there's a . . . fib!

Alternating between lyrical and dramatic moments, between various types of irony, "Araby" anticipates the modulation of epiphany and deflation found in *A Portrait of the Artist as a Young Man*. Early in the story, the narrator experiences his vision of Mangan's sister as an epiphany calling his soul forth to adventure. Like the deflations in *Portrait*, the final passage explicitly revises, and at least partially discounts, the validity of the original epiphany.

Similar complexities occur in many other stories. Even in the early story "Eveline," Frank and Eveline experience contradictory epiphanies: Eveline's urge for escape collapses into the paralysis articulated in Frank's (or perhaps the narrator's) epiphany in which she is revealed to be a trapped animal. In "The Sisters," the closing image of Father Flynn sitting "wide-awake and laughing-like to himself" reads very much like an epiphany. But it is not clear whether the core of the epiphany is Father Flynn's recognition of the emptiness of his religion and/or his religious vocation; the sisters' realization that Father Flynn has gone mad; or the boy's realization of the corruption of a society in which the dead priest is subjected to innuendo and unfounded speculation. Like the gradual psychologizing of Joyce's "scrupulously mean" style, the increasing complexity of his epiphanies is basic to the mature voice capable of articulating the contingent experience of truth as an ongoing process for character, author/narrator, and reader.

· 6 ·

"THE DEAD":
PROCESS AND SYMPATHY

Universally recognized as Joyce's finest short story, "The Dead" marks a culmination and an extension of the central stylistic and thematic concerns of *Dubliners*. Like "The Sisters," "The Dead" focuses on the interrelationship of the living and the dead; it has been observed that the titles of Joyce's opening and closing stories are interchangeable. Although the extent of his sympathy remains an open question, Joyce's decision to end *Dubliners* with "The Dead" certainly reflects a more sympathetic view of Ireland than his original plan to conclude with the simoniac priest of "Grace." Acknowledging the paralysis of Dublin life, the corruption of Irish institutions, and the limitations of the characters' language, "The Dead" develops the implications of these situations in a fuller, more psychologically complex manner than any earlier story.

Despite this complexity, a general consensus has developed concerning the basic elements of "The Dead." The story's power rests on Joyce's treatment of Gabriel Conroy, a university teacher and writer of a newspaper literary column. Although Little Chandler, James Duffy, and the narrators of the first three stories share aspects of Gabriel's character, none is developed in equivalent depth. As he interacts first with the various guests at his aunts' Christmas party and later with his wife, Gretta, Gabriel slowly comes to his own realization of several of Joyce's central themes. Afflicted by the solipsism that traps Duffy, unable to follow through on his inchoate urges for escape, Gabriel recognizes his own paralysis. Moving beyond the relatively simple despair reflected in the conclusions of "Araby" and "A Painful Case," the final epiphany of the snow falling across Ireland expresses Gabriel's very Joycean perception of paralysis as an ambiguous link between its victims, urban and rural, living and dead. Offering at least a tentative hope of rebirth, this epiphany, more than any other passage in *Dubliners*, asserts the general, and perhaps universal, dimension of Joyce's vision of the specifically Irish malaise.

Joyce structures "The Dead" around Gabriel's egoistic responses to the events at and after the party. Set in a more affluent social milieu than any earlier story—the sisters can afford "diamond-bone sirloins, three-shilling tea and the best bottled stout"—the party reflects the paralysis delineated in the first fourteen stories. In addition, however, it reflects Joyce's desire, expressed in a letter to Stanislaus, to mitigate the "unnecessarily harsh" vision by acknowledging his home country's "ingenuous insularity and its hospitality." The familial connections and ritualistic qualities of the gathering, which takes place on the Feast of the Epiphany (6 January) at the end of the Christmas season, soften Joyce's portrait of extreme isolation or meaningless public contact. Most of the characters seem to enjoy the event. Gabriel's speech celebrating Ireland's "spirit of good-fellowship" should not be dismissed too rapidly. The food and drink are abundant; Gabriel's speech provides a fitting climax to the dinner, whatever its implications in regard to his internal processes. While many characters are satirized mildly, Joyce portrays none as harshly as he does Jimmy Doyle, James Duffy, or Father Purdon. At best, the party provides a setting for potentially meaningful exchanges such as the conversation between Molly Ivors and Gabriel, or Freddy Malins's response to Aunt Julia's singing.

This is not to say that Joyce celebrates Irish hospitality in any simplistic manner. Paralysis and death hover over the party. The characters present or referred to in the story can be classified as physically dead (Gabriel's mother, the two Patrick Morkans, Michael Furey); near to death (Aunt Julia, Aunt Kate, Mrs. Malins); or living dead, a category that includes all the remaining characters to a lesser or greater degree. As he had done in the stories of public life, Joyce re-iterates the failure of politics, religion, and art to provide any meaningful outlet for the impulses that glimmer through the party. Although Irish nationalism elicits a passionate response from Molly Ivors, Joyce images political paralysis in the snow-covered statue of the liberator, Daniel O'Connell. Reflecting his lack of political awareness, Gabriel writes for the conservative *Daily Express*, justifying his actions with the thought that "literature was above politics."

Reduced to a source of parlor talk, religion provides no wider outlet for creative energy. Although religious imagery permeates "The Dead," the characters' religious discourse extends no further than speculation on the monks who "never spoke, got up at two in the morning and slept in their coffins." Although the image reinforces the themes of death and paralysis, it has no factual basis, thereby highlighting the theological shallowness of Catholic Dublin. Given the fact that Gabriel's brother is a priest whose church lies less than twenty-five miles from his aunts' residence, the absence of priests from the party seems particularly striking. Although the absence is not explained, it may reflect Kate's bitterness over Pope Pius X's declaration that choir positions were liturgical offices, thus rendering them inaccessible to women and forcing Julia to give up her position in Father Healy's church.

Like politics and religion, art provides no real alternative to the stultifying atmosphere, an especially telling failure given the musical vocations of several characters. When Mary Jane plays "her Academy piece," Gabriel thinks "the piece she was playing had no melody for him and he doubted whether it had any melody for the other listeners." Montaged with the enthusiastic, but hypocritical, applause from the young men who left the room during the recital, this passage reveals the Dubliners' substitution of technique for feeling, reiterated in the conversational focus on performers rather than composers. In addition, it suggests the unwillingness of even the more aware members of the audience, such as Gabriel, to seek anything other than a superficially appealing aesthetic experience (the exclusive emphasis on melody). As in the other stories in *Dubliners,* the absence of an adequate language, reflected in the preponderance of repetition and cliché in conversation, reinforces the institutional paralysis.

GABRIEL'S PROCESS

Capable of recognizing most of these problems, Gabriel perceives himself as superior to his surroundings. Adopting a condescending tone toward his aunts—he thinks of the "Graces of Dublin" as "two ignorant old women"—Gabriel worries that the Browning quotation he plans to use in his speech will surpass his audience's aesthetic capacity. Despite these feelings, however, Gabriel spends much of the evening worrying that he will appear foolish, that others secretly condescend to him. Gabriel's obsessive concern with his public image renders him vulnerable to seemingly trivial disturbances, particularly those involving women. Relatively at ease in the masculine world, Gabriel responds weakly, or not at all, when his perceptions are disputed first by Lily, then by Molly Ivors, and finally by his wife. Coming in response to Gabriel's social raillery, Lily's bitter comment that "The men that is now is only all palaver and what they can get out of you" implicates Gabriel with the "common" people he feels are beneath him.

Contrasting with his self-defined "defeats" at the hands of Lily ("he felt he had made a mistake") and Molly Ivors ("She had tried to make him ridiculous before people"), Gabriel experiences several moments of triumph. Both his speech and his retelling of the story of Johnny the horse heighten his sense of satisfaction. Watching Gretta listen to Bartell D'Arcy's singing, Gabriel leaves the party with a feeling of aesthetic exhilaration despite the earlier disruptions. As Gabriel and Gretta return to the hotel where they will spend the night away from their children, Gabriel feels intense sexual desire and envisions a romantic climax to the evening. Completing the pattern of egoistic triumph and equally egoistic defeat, Gabriel's fantasy collapses in the face of Gretta's actual experience. D'Arcy's song—"The Lass of Aughrim"—turns Gretta's thoughts toward Michael Furey, who had courted her during her youth in the west of Ireland. Acutely disappointed and jealous of the shadowy Michael, Gabriel can do little save listen and wait for his wife to fall asleep. In a story populated by an abundance of ghosts—of singers, King William, Daniel O'Connell, the two Patrick Morkans, Gabriel's mother Ellen—the dead youth is more real to the Conroys than any living person.

As Gretta sleeps beside him, Gabriel experiences an epiphany of his own connection with the living dead. One of the most famous concluding passages in modern literature, Gabriel's epiphany reflects his weariness at the end of a long and emotionally exhausting day. Like the conclusions of "Araby" and "A Painful Case," Gabriel's epiphany reflects his sudden awareness of his own egoism. Unlike Duffy or the disillusioned youth, however, Gabriel places this recognition in the context of a widening circle of connections:

> The time had come for him to set out on his journey westward. Yes, the newspapers were right: snow was general all over Ireland. It was falling on every part of the dark central plain, on the treeless hills, falling softly upon the Bog of Allen and, farther westward, softly falling into the dark mutinous Shannon waves. It was falling, too, upon every part of the lonely churchyard on the hill where Michael Furey lay buried. It lay thickly drifted on the crooked crosses and headstones, on the spears of the little gate, on the barren thorns. His soul swooned slowly as he heard the snow falling faintly through the universe and faintly falling, like the descent of their last end, upon all the living and the dead.

One in a sequence of epiphanies occurring toward the end of "The Dead," this passage is written in the mature style Joyce had perfected during the writing of *Dubliners*. The story's effectiveness hinges on Joyce's ability to establish both close sympathy and ironic distance between the reader and Gabriel. He accomplishes this delicate balance through a gradually accelerating dramatic rhythm combined with subtle modulations in the style of individual sentences. "The Dead" can be divided into five or six sections, each consisting of several scenes. Beginning with Gabriel's arrival and the musical entertainment (which can be viewed either as a single section or as two distinct sections), Joyce establishes a fairly leisurely pace, shifting slowly from scene to scene and character to character. Although Gabriel emerges as the central character, he does not dominate the action. The sentence structure of the opening section reflects this relatively diffuse focus. In accord with the "Uncle Charles Principle," the style of the opening sentence— "Lily, the caretaker's daughter, was literally run off her feet"—is connected with Lily more strongly than with Gabriel who, as a "literary" man, would be unlikely to declare the figurative phrase "run off her feet" to be "literal." Before coming to focus on Gabriel at the beginning of the sixth paragraph, the style juxtaposes several perspectives: Lily's, the Misses Morkan's, and the general social perspective reflected in the exaggerations of the second paragraph: "It was *always a great affair. . . . Everybody* who knew them came to it. . . . *Never once* had it fallen flat. For *years and years* it had gone off in *splendid* style." Again reflecting the Uncle Charles Principle, the scene between Gabriel and Lily establishes the characteristic attitude, tone, and vocabulary of Gabriel's introspection: "He was still discomposed by the girl's bitter and sudden retort. . . . He was undecided about the lines from Browning for he feared they would be above the heads of his hearers." Carefully reiterating the distance between narrative perspective and Gabriel, Joyce returns to several other characters including Mr. Browne and Freddy Malins near the close of the section.

Having established the flexibility of the narrative voice, Joyce focuses more clearly on Gabriel during the second section, which opens with his reflections on Mary Jane's recital. Extending the characteristic rhythm of confidence and deflation established during the scene with Lily, Joyce presents Gabriel's conversation with Molly Ivors entirely from Gabriel's perspective. Even the momentary shift to the neighbors who "had turned to listen to the cross-examination" reflects Gabriel's defensive concern with his public image. The third section consists largely of a description of the food (perhaps reflecting the social voice of the first section) and the direct quotation of Gabriel's speech. Combined with the leisurely dramatic pace—no scene shifts occur during the dinner—the withdrawal from Gabriel's internal responses reestablishes the distinction between Gabriel's perspective and the narrative voice.

As the dinner ends and the characters begin to depart, the dramatic rhythm accelerates rapidly and the narrative voice begins to align more clearly with Gabriel. Focusing on the departures, the fourth section consists of five relatively brief scenes. The fifth, focusing on Gabriel and Gretta in their room, consists of two scenes, much more intimate and narrowly focused than anything preceeding them. Both in Gabriel's vision of Gretta on the stairs and in his vision of "their secret life together," which "burst like stars upon his memory," Joyce attaches the style almost entirely to Gabriel's perspective. Echoing his exhilaration, the sentences register only what Gabriel thinks, sees, or feels. Even the external events that interrupt his revery are presented from Gabriel's perspective: "At the corner of Winetavern Street they met a cab. He was glad of its rattling noise as it saved him from conversation." Similarly, the scene between Gretta and Gabriel in the hotel diminishes the ironic potential of the narrative voice, reporting Gabriel's perceptions in Gabriel's characteristic voice: "He saw himself as a ludicrous figure. . . . A vague terror seized Gabriel at this answer as if, at that hour when he had hoped to triumph, some impalpable and vindictive being was coming against him, gathering forces against him in its vague world." In the climactic vision of the snow, the narrative voice invites the reader to participate in Gabriel's responses much more directly than in any previous scene.

As a result, it is difficult to gauge the distance between character and narrator. Yet such distance, qualitatively different from that in "Araby" or "A Painful Case," is basic to a comprehensive reading of Gabriel's final epiphany, either as ironic commentary on the character who experiences the epiphany as the end of a process; or on the narrator/reader who may share Gabriel's uncritical reaction or (less likely) adopt a position of aloof superiority. A reading of Gabriel's vision as the culmination of a process acknowledges that it is only one of several epiphanies, or near epiphanies, presented near the end of "The Dead." As a sequence, these epiphanies suggest a process of exhilaration and deflation in Gabriel's thoughts, an oscillation recalling Joyce's ironic treatment of Stephen Dedalus's epiphanies in *A Portrait of the Artist as a Young Man*. Viewing Gretta on the stairs, Gabriel meditates on the question "what is a woman standing on the stairs in the shadow, listening to distant music, a symbol of." Although the moment could well provide the material for a lyrical revelation, Gabriel's rational answer—"*Distant Music* he would call the picture if he were a painter"—effectively drains its epiphanic potential. Still, Gabriel's imagination has been engaged. As he walks behind Gretta, he remembers a past scene in terms closely resembling the dramatic epiphanies:

> He was standing with her in the cold, looking in through a grated window at a man making bottles in a roaring furnace. It was very cold. Her face, fragrant in the cold air, was quite close to his; and suddenly she called out to the man at the furnace:
> —Is the fire hot, sir?

Although this epiphany is rich in possible meaning—the imagery can be seen as infernal, passionate, mundane—Gabriel retreats, observing the bottlemaker's lack of an answer "was just as well. He might have answered rudely." Shortly thereafter, envisioning the return to the hotel, Gabriel imagines a scene reminiscent of the lyrical epiphanies:

> He would call her softly:
> —Gretta!
> Perhaps she would not hear at once: she would be undressing. Then something in his voice would strike her. She would turn and look at him.

Again, however, this epiphany breaks off, interrupted by the rattling noise of the cab.

Reported in a voice as closely aligned with Gabriel's as that of the final vision of the snow, these near epiphanies occur in an ongoing process. Each moment takes its meaning from the rhythm and content of the events that surround it, including previous epiphanies or potential epiphanies. The exhilarating—or the damning—insights of one moment may decay into the crushing ironies of the next. What is most important to realize, however, is that Joyce does not limit this insight to Gabriel. No longer does he claim an objective perspective such as that in the harsh dramatic epiphany that concludes "Counterparts." Nor does he assume an ironic perspective such as that which enabled him to undercut James Duffy's lyrical epiphany in "A Painful Case." By surrendering the carefully established stylistic distance of the first sections and merging his narrative voice with Gabriel's, Joyce acknowledges his own participation in the process of revelation and collapse. Tempering the harshness of the earlier stories, Joyce suggests that all moments of epiphany—including his own, whether lyrical or dramatic—should be viewed as simultaneously serious—the truths of the moment—and subject to revision. This takes on special importance in relation to the final vision. Recognizing the validity of Gabriel's sense of his own paralysis, Joyce nonetheless suggests that he has made a substantial advance when he interprets that paralysis as an emblem of a shared burden. Marking Joyce's final departure from the concept of the epiphany suggested in the notebooks and employed in the early stories of *Dubliners*, "The Dead" embraces process as the point of connection between character, author, and reader, between "all the living and the dead."

ALTERNATIVE APPROACHES

With the possible exception of the section concerning Gabriel's sequence of epiphanies, the preceeding discussion reflects a general consensus on "The Dead." Assuming only the knowledge available to most first-time readers, it incorporates stylistic and thematic perceptions shared by most critics. Drawing on a wide range of background information and critical techniques, these critics elaborate on the basic reading in diverse ways. Many have uncovered multiple layers of meaning that necessitate some adjustment in the way the basic elements of "The Dead" are understood. Frequently, the submerged patterns are brought to focus on Gabriel's closing epiphany, shifting the relative emphasis placed on the themes of paralysis/isolation and connection/rebirth. Some frames of reference reinforce patterns of meaning apparent on the surface; some necessitate only minor adjustments; a few require major reversals of apparent meaning. Joyce most certainly incorporated a great deal of symbolic and suggestive material into "The Dead." Like *Dubliners* as a whole, the story supplies evidence for almost every critical approach. Resisting the imposition of a single determined meaning, Joyce provides a field of play for various interpretive processes, challenging his readers to incorporate even the seemingly contradictory aspects of experience.

Biographically based approaches to "The Dead" generally require relatively little adjustment of thematic readings, whatever their emphasis. Some amount to little more than curiosities. Noting Joyce's early interest in cinema—he was involved in opening Dublin's first movie theater—Paul Deane has suggested that the accelerating rhythm of scenes parallels standard motion picture rhythm. While this may explain John Huston's interest in filming the story, it seems unlikely, given the primitive stage of cinematic aesthetics during the first decade of the century, that Joyce actually had such a point of reference in mind. More significantly, Richard Ellmann has demonstrated in minute detail the biographical sources of the story's characters and locales. Aunt Julia and Aunt Kate are based on Joyce's great-aunts Mrs. Callanan and Mrs. Lyons, who lived at 15 Usher's Island along with Mrs. Callanan's daughter Mary Ellen, the model for Mary Jane. Most of the guests at the party, which resembles the ones his family attended during Joyce's youth, are also based on actual Dubliners. More significant in relation to the interpretation of "The Dead" are the models for Gabriel Conroy. These include Joyce's father, who presided over the festive dinners; Joyce's friend Constantine Curran, who shares Gabriel's mannerisms and interest in European travel; and Joyce himself, whose relationship with Nora Barnacle informs the Conroy marriage.

The relationship of Michael Furey and Gretta Conroy clearly derives from a similar incident involving Nora and Michael "Sonny" Bodkin, a young man who courted Nora in Galway. Like Furey, Bodkin died shortly after he left his sickroom to visit Nora. There seems little doubt that Joyce, who suffered intermittently from jealous rages, shared Gabriel's sensitivity to betrayal, a sensitivity grounded in his feeling that his wife failed to adequately distinguish him from other men. This in turn suggests several distinctly speculative biographical connections between Gabriel and Joyce. If Joyce shares Gabriel's sense of unrecognized superiority, is it legitimate to see Gabriel, as several critics have, as a comment on what would have happened to Joyce if he remained in Ireland? A frustrated creative writer who expresses himself only in sterile academic forms, Gabriel could be seen as succumbing to the paralysis from which Joyce had escaped. Emphasizing the Gabriel-Joyce connection could result in various adjustments of thematic understanding. On one hand, Joyce could be seen as assuming a position of superiority based on his ability to escape the snares that entrap Gabriel. On the other, the connection could be seen as a means of elevating Gabriel by emphasizing the creative potential of his final imaginative transformation of mundane materials, which in general terms recalls a Joycean epiphany. While recognizing the biographical sources of various characters does provide fascinating insights into Joyce's creative process, on balance the biographical references offer little support to any particular thematic approach.

Approaches emphasizing patterns of imagery or allusion are generally less neutral in their impact. "The Dead" reiterates several image patterns that are present throughout *Dubliners*. Among the most important are the symbolic oppositions of movement-enclosure, darkness-light, and warmth-cold. Directions, colors, and the elements, particularly water in its various forms, possess clear symbolic dimensions. In the early stories, most of the symbols cluster around the underlying opposition between life (movement, light, warmth) and death (enclosure, darkness, cold). Not surprisingly, statistical analyses have demonstrated conclusively the preponderance of "negative" symbols; most of the stories are set late in the day, in cold weather, etc. In "The Dead," however, Joyce's use of the symbols is more complex. Where in the previous stories symbolic meaning rested on traditional meanings combined with the narrator's judgment of the situation, symbolic meaning in "The Dead" incorporates associations derived from the characters' past experiences.

"The Dead"

Exploiting the potential for symbolic ambiguity inherent in this tension, Joyce structures the conclusion of "The Dead" around a cluster of symbols that revise the traditional meanings invoked earlier in *Dubliners*. The symbolic crux of the epiphany lies in the combination of the snow and Gabriel's westward journey. As Brewster Ghiselin observes in an essay that established the basic symbolic approach to *Dubliners*, Joyce typically images the west as a place of death and entrapment contrasting with the "symbolic orient" associated with rebirth and escape. Particularly when associated with the snow, which in conventional terms represents the water of life in a frozen (paralyzed) form, the westward movement supports a reading of Gabriel's vision as a despairing revelation of the spiritual death awaiting those who remain in Ireland. As Ghiselin recognizes, however, several factors—one concerning the meaning of the snow, the other of the west—mitigate this reading. When the specific associations of the west for Gabriel and Gretta are taken into account, it can no longer be seen purely as a symbol of death. For Gretta, the west represents the more intense life of her youth. Although Gabriel's associations with the west differ from his wife's, Joyce's treatment implies an underlying connection. Uncomfortable with passion, Gabriel avoids the west, refusing to consider seriously Molly Ivors's suggestion of an Irish vacation. Far from representing a movement to the spiritual rebirth traditionally associated with the East, Gabriel's preference for the continent both reiterates his feeling of superiority and emphasizes his alienation from Gretta. His final imaginative movement toward the west partially mitigates these tendencies. If the west remains a place of death—as the cemeteries of the final vision underline—it is now a death associated with a shared fate, increasing rather than reducing compassion.

Joyce's manipulation of snow imagery, which reflects Gabriel's psychology, reinforces this adjustment of conventional symbolic meanings. In part, this also reflects meanings grounded in Gabriel's psychology. Feeling trapped by the party, Gabriel frequently attributes positive characteristics to traditionally negative images: he sees Gretta standing in the shadows; he remembers standing with her in the cold; he asks the porter in the hotel to remove the candle. Juxtaposed with the enclosure of the party, the snow too has idiosyncratic meaning for Gabriel. More important to Joyce's treatment of the image, however, is his invocation of an implicit level of meaning. Gabriel's vision concludes with the snow "softly falling into the dark mutinous Shannon waves." Combining Gretta's positive vision of the west with a suggestion of a potentially rebellious Irish political energy (the "mutinous Shannon waves"), the image intimates the melting of the frozen snow into the life-giving water. Far from a surrender to death, Gabriel's journey to a snowy west metamorphoses into a liberating movement toward symbolic rebirth.

In addition to the conventional and psychological approaches, a number of specific frames of reference have been used to clarify the symbolic structures of "The Dead." Several critics emphasize the significance of Christian references, particularly those involving the epiphany season and the angels Gabriel and Michael. As Florence Walzl observes, Joyce employs the contrast between the archangel Michael and the angel Gabriel to reinforce the ambiguities of the final epiphany. Traditionally imaged as the "Prince of Snow," Michael is associated with water and the last judgment. Associated with the element of fire, Gabriel is the angel of the annunciation. Juxtaposing the angelic avatars of new eras and merging their elemental associations— the angel of fire accepts his bond with the angel of water/snow—Joyce reinforces the sense of the ending as a time of conciliation and potential rebirth. By setting his story on 6 January, the Feast of the Epiphany, Joyce suggests parallels between the realistic action and the manifestation of Christ's divinity. As with most symbolic glosses, the references to the epiphany can be understood with varying degrees of irony. Emphasizing the theme of paralysis, Julian Kaye identifies an intricate parody of the marriage at Cana (the scene between Gabriel and Lily), the visit of the Magi (the dance), and baptisim of Christ (Gabriel's hopes for a new life). Reiterating the ironic understanding of the epiphany season in "The Dead," Bernard Benstock perceives a more complex symbolic strategy. An ineffectual representative of the Magi—he comes from the east with a gift of gold for Lily, the embittered symbol of the Virgin Mary—Gabriel ultimately acknowledges paralysis, his own and that of Christianity. His final epiphany marks the beginning of his journey toward a threatening spiritual rebirth comparable to that in W. B. Yeats's poem "The Second Coming."

Although Yeats had not yet written his poem when Joyce wrote "The Dead," several critics have sought insights in other Irish materials. Some Irish references simply clarify Joyce's use of sources. Ellmann traces the imagery of the final paragraph to George Moore's novel *Vain Fortune*. Other allusions, such as that to "The Lass of Aughrim," increase the emotional depth of certain passages. A song about a young girl in the west of Ireland who, seduced and abandoned, drowns herself, "The Lass of Aughrim" reinforces the imagery of isolation and betrayal that develops through the final sections. In contrast with these informational glosses, some Irish allusions suggest more specific interpretations. Tracing many of the details in the concluding passages of "The Dead" to Yeats's *Stories of Red Hanrahan*, John Paul Riquelme emphasizes Joyce's embrace of the Irish tradition, lending support to a positive reading of the closing westward movement. John Kelleher bases his understanding of Gabriel's character in part on an intricate reading of the parallel between "The Dead" and the Irish epic "The Destruction of Da Derga's Hostel." The story of a good king who brings about his own undoing by violating several taboos, the epic provides a symbolic substructure for Gabriel's problems at the party. More convincing is Kelleher's demonstration that many of the details in "The Dead" invoke aspects of Dublin history. Citing details such as the association of Back Lane (where Gabriel's grandfather kept a starch mill) with Catholic resistance to English domination, Kelleher argues convincingly that Gabriel inadvertently, but repeatedly, sins against the memory of the Irish dead. While this does not necessitate any major shift in understanding of the ending, the presence of the Irish allusions certainly adds another dimension to Gabriel's character.

Reinforcing this reading of Gabriel's failings, one of the most fascinating approaches to the symbolism of "The Dead," presented both by Kelleher and by Roger Cox, focuses on the story of Patrick Morkan and his horse, the "never-to-be-forgotten Johnny." Presented as an amusing anecdote, Gabriel's story concerns a horse, trained to walk in circles to power Patrick Morkan's mill. Taken out to attend a military review, Johnny proceeds until he reaches the statue of William III of England. Gabriel concludes the anecdote: "and whether he fell in love with the horse King Billy sits on or whether he thought he was back again in the mill, anyhow he began to walk round the statue. . . . Round and round he went . . . and the old gentleman, who was a very pompous old gentleman, was highly indignant. *Go on, sir! What do you mean, sir? Johnny! Johnny! Most extraordinary conduct! Can't understand the horse!*". Removed in 1929 after it had been twice blown up by Irish nationalists, the statue of William, who defeated the Irish at Aughrim in 1691, clearly invokes the theme of political paralysis. Arguing that the horse's politically inappropriate behavior elicits Patrick Morkan's quite appropriate dismay, Kelleher concludes that Gabriel is simply unaware of his political heritage. Taking a psychological approach to the story, Cox identifies the anecdote as the actual epiphany of "The Dead," the trivial incident that illuminates and integrates other meanings. Associating Gretta with Johnny, and Gabriel (who treats his wife as a horse) with Patrick, Cox identifies Michael as the psychic monument around which the Conroys circle aimlessly. Yet another reading of the anecdote might combine these two approaches, arguing that Patrick's failure to understand Johnny, like Gabriel's failure to understand Gretta, stems from his inability to understand his own implication in the oppressive system. Having attained a substantial measure of financial success based on the labor of his horse and his willingness to coexist with the British authorities, Patrick should not be shocked by Johnny's reversion to the only pattern of behavior he has ever known. Similarly, Gabriel's failure to articulate the point of the anecdote represents a parallel refusal to acknowledge his own contribution to the paralysis that contributes to Gretta's seemingly inexplicable behavior.

As this reading implies, shifting focus within the story may reveal possible meanings analogous to those revealed by the use of new frames of reference. While most readings of "The Dead" focus narrowly on Gabriel, it is possible to decenter the text by granting an equivalent attention to the experiences of "marginal" characters such as Lily, Freddy Malins, or, most important, Gretta Conroy. Taken seriously, Lily's claim that "The men that is now is only all palaver and what they can get out of you" comments with disturbing accuracy on Gabriel. Covering his lack of understanding of women with small talk such as the comment that elicits Lily's response, Gabriel's disillusionment in the final section results in part from the frustration of his sexual desires. Similarly, although Freddy Malins is usually dismissed as a drunk who has been unable to honor his pledge of sobriety for even a week, he is the only character who shows any real aesthetic appreciation. The sincere enthusiasm of his response to Aunt Julia's singing—"when he could clap no more, he stood up suddenly and hurried across the room to Aunt Julia whose hand he seized and held in both his hands, shaking it when words failed him or the catch in his voice proved too much for him"—contrasts sharply with Gabriel's flowery, but empty, tribute to his aunt as one of the Graces of Dublin.

Focusing on Gretta provides further insight into Gabriel's character. Most critics assume that Gabriel is correct in believing Michael Furey to have been Gretta's great lost love. Yet there is little evidence in her speech to support such an interpretation. She refers to him repeatedly as a "poor fellow," a "boy." Uncomprehending when Gabriel suggests that her desire to visit the west of Ireland is grounded in her desire to revisit the scene of her lost love, she says nothing which indicates that she took Furey seriously as a suitor, even in her youth. Inspired by an openly sentimental song that focuses on the death of a young girl, Gretta's "epiphany" focuses on her own lost youth, not on the young boy who Gabriel sees as a rival for her love. Particularly when viewed as a group, these insights from the margins of "The Dead" emphasize the depth of Gabriel's solipsism. Although it focuses almost exclusively on Gabriel, Edward Brandabur's psychoanalytical reading leads to a similar conclusion. Stressing Gabriel's "neurotic passivity" and drawing attention to related details such as his interest in two death-oriented pictures (of Romeo and Juliet and the two princes murdered by Richard III), Brandabur concludes that Gabriel's final stance is at least implicitly sadomasochistic, a punishment for disobeying his mother's opposition to the marriage with Gretta.

This brief application of alternative approaches to "The Dead" by no means exhausts the possibilities. Critics have explored references to operas, Browning, the *Iliad,* and classical mythology (the

Three Graces of Dublin). Aware of Joyce's interest in Dante, others have identified the party as hell, the carriage ride as purgatory, and the hotel room as a somewhat ironic paradise. An examination of references to American literature reveals a major source in Bret Harte's novel *Gabriel Conroy*, which also concerns a snowbound party including two lovers. It seems likely that Joyce, who enjoyed paradox and ambiguity, especially when it reinforced the image of his own genius, was aware of most of these levels of meaning in "The Dead." Rather than seeking to establish a hierarchy of reading, which the very proliferation of systems resists, the story, like *Dubliners* as a whole, invites the reader to resist the urge for simplification, to develop a reading process capable of balancing their sometimes contradictory implications.

· 7 ·

CONSTRUCTING JOYCES

As the preceeding reading of "The Dead" suggests, *Dubliners* provides material for the construction of a large, perhaps unlimited, number of "James Joyces." By focusing on a particular type of material, or assuming a particular critical perspective, a reader can provide convincing evidence that a particular James Joyce actually exists. Focusing on his use of verifiable historical materials can create an image of Joyce as an objective chronicler of Irish social conditions. Focusing on references to Catholicism can create an image of Joyce as an essentially theological writer. A detailed analysis of the interlocking image patterns and verbal echoes in the text suggests that Joyce was primarily concerned with prose style per se. The list can be extended indefinitely. What is important is that each approach is particular, a way of apprehending specific aspects of a more complex phenomenon that assumes its full (and unparaphrasable) meaning only as a whole. The claims of any particular approach should not be exaggerated. Each highlights a particular group of tensions in *Dubliners,* raising questions and clarifying issues that might be invisible or inexplicable from another perspective. The cost of such triumphs, however, is almost inevitably the exclusion or marginalization of other questions and issues.

Each of the following sections constructs an image of a particular "James Joyce." Some of these approaches are quite narrow, creating limited (but not entirely invalid) images; some combine related approaches to construct more elaborate (but still partial) images. Each construction can be viewed as an attempt to explain what *Dubliners* is "really" about. Critiquing the limitations of the previous image, each subsequent image contradicts or extends that explanation. This counter-image is then subjected to similar treatment. While it would be possible to play this game forever, the point is to demonstrate the limitations of any simplifying approach to the field of play Joyce provides in *Dubliners*. This method of presenting a particular approach to reality and then demonstrating its limitations parallels Joyce's rhetorical strategy and thematic intent. Critiquing a society paralyzed by its commitments to various systems of thought and/or institutions that force the repression of aspects of reality, Joyce invites his readers to engage in an analogous process. Offering a variety of limited, and limiting, perspectives on his materials, Joyce forces his readers to come to terms with the inevitable limitations of their own sense-making process.

JOYCE AS AUTOBIOGRAPHICAL WRITER

Although *Dubliners* is clearly not an autobiography, Joyce made extensive use of his own experience in crafting the book. As James Olney observes, the term *autobiography* is derived from three root words, each of which implies a different analytical focus. The root *autos* highlights the importance of the *self*, usually the self that reflects back on previous events; *bios* focuses on the life being recounted, the events themselves; *graphia* focuses on the writing process that transmits the other elements. Extending the conventional understanding of autobiography, Olney's analysis can be applied to *Dubliners* in several ways. Documenting the specifically autobiographical sources of characters and events, especially when Joyce alters verifiable details, can provide insight into his thematic or stylistic intentions. Examining the underlying concerns reflected in Joyce's life can help identify patterns that might otherwise remain veiled. While such approaches can illuminate various aspects of Joyce's psyche, most focus on what was probably the central concern of his early life: his developing sense of himself as an artistic exile seeking to transform a recalcitrant reality into meaningful art.

Focusing on the *bios,* and drawing heavily on the source material provided in Richard Ellmann's masterful biography *James Joyce,* it is relatively easy to catalog actual events used in *Dubliners.* Some of these were drawn from Joyce's childhood experiences. Set in the house at 17 North Richmond Street, where the Joyce family moved in 1894, "Araby" makes use of a bazaar that came to Dublin in May of that year. Based on an actual expedition shared by Joyce and Stanislaus, "An Encounter" re-creates the brothers' meeting with a homosexual. Numerous characters in *Dubliners* are modelled on Joyce's acquaintances: Molly Ivors on Kathleen Sheehy; Mr. Kernan in "Grace" on Ned Thornton; the title character of "Eveline" on Thornton's daughter Eveline. On occasion, Joyce uses names to take revenge against people who had crossed members of his family. The abusive Mr. Alleyne in "Counterparts" recalls Henry Alleyn, who had bilked John Joyce years earlier in a business deal. Similarly, Joyce gave the central character of "A Painful Case" the last name Duffy after "Pisser Duffy," who had fought with Stanislaus. The latter example is particularly instructive since the primary source of Duffy's character is Stanislaus himself, whose diary provided Joyce with the general outline for the story.

While numerous such details of Joyce's *bios* have been identified, focusing on the *autos*—the self—in *Dubliners* raises more interesting questions concerning the text's expression of the recurring obsessions of Joyce's life. His identification with Parnell and his obsessive distrust of friends, for example, cast light on the theme of betrayal. A leitmotif in Joyce's biography, this theme recurs throughout *Dubliners* in varied forms: Corley's betrayal of the slavey in "Two Gallants"; Gretta's imagined betrayal of Gabriel in "The Dead," which reverberates with Joyce's own concern over Nora's relationships with past lovers, real or imagined. The ending of "Eveline," where the young woman pulls back from her lover, may reflect the anxiety Joyce felt over the possibility that Nora might not go through with their elopement. While not autobiographical in a literal sense, *Dubliners* is clearly the production of a self with an idiosyncratic set of recurring interests and obsessions.

The most rewarding autobiographical approach to *Dubliners*, however, focuses on *graphia*, Joyce's awareness of writing as the means of mediating between and (re)creating life and self. Viewing *Dubliners* as a kind of diffused "Portrait of the Artist," this approach can focus either on individual stories as Joyce's meditations on particular phases of his own life, or on structural patterns reflecting the dominant motif of that life: his own artistic maturation. If Joyce exists as character in *Dubliners,* it is in the first three stories, all of which are narrated in the first person by unnamed young boys. Some critics interpret these three narrators as one character, explicitly or implicitly identified with the young James Joyce or his fictional alter-ego Stephen Dedalus. While details such as the North Richmond Street address firmly establish a relationship between Joyce and his narrators, other significant details distinguish the three narrators from their creator and from one another. The narrator of "The Sisters" seems distinctly more passive than the narrator of "An Encounter," who defies authority by playing truant. Although the possibilities are abundant, Joyce does nothing to emphasize a connection between the sexual fascination of the narrators of "An Encounter" (who is both repelled and fascinated by the pervert) and "Araby" (who views himself as a romantic supplicant). Distinguishing the boys from Joyce himself is the fact that two of the narrators live with aunts and uncles rather than parents. It is possible, of course, that Joyce altered the detail to emphasize his feeling of alienation, his familial experience of betrayal. But the fact that he did not do so in *Stephen Hero,* which he was writing contemporaneously with *Dubliners,* cautions against too strong an assertion of autobiographical identification.

This does not, however, deny the general parallel between the author and his sensitive young narrators, each of whom confronts pressures similar to those Joyce confronted in his own youth. If any of the boys are to survive with their creative energies intact, they will need to find a way to defend their perceptions against external pressures. Like Joyce, they will have to resist the paralyzing claims of country, church, and family. While the escape attempts portrayed in *Dubliners* may be simplistic, they intimate the Joycean values of "silence, exile and cunning." As Judith Montgomery suggests in her essay on the importance of silence in *Dubliners,* the narrator of "The Sisters" embodies the principle of silence, which he sees as a refuge from adult coarseness; the narrator of "An Encounter" is deeply repelled by the corruption of the word (a corruption he begins to internalize when he assumes a false name); and the narrator of "Araby" consciously chooses silence after his attempt to communicate with the girl at the bazaar fails. The structural pattern that isolates the young narrators' first person voices from the relatively impersonal third person voices of their elders implies the necessity of learning to make effective use of protective silence. If they fail to do so, Joyce implies, the boys will soon be indistinguishable from the crushed characters of the later stories.

Extending patterns established in the stories of youth, "A Little Cloud," "A Painful Case," and "The Dead" complete Joyce's gallery of "self-portraits" in *Dubliners.* Each concerns the fate of an artist, or would be artist, who fails to develop adequate defenses. Devoid of creative outlet, Little Chandler falls into a tormenting and pointless envy of Ignatius Gallaher; James Duffy retreats into a self-deluded sense of superiority; Gabriel Conroy begins to realize the nature of his dilemma only at the end of "The Dead." In each case, Joyce's meditations on the fate of the imagination in Dublin provides further support and justification for his own decision—which he was reaching as he wrote the stories—to fly beyond the nets of his native land.

Each of these autobiographical approaches raises questions concerning the rhetorical relationship between Joyce, his narrative voice, and his characters. One approach to this question, stressing Joyce's developing recognition that he shared his characters' dilemmas, has been sketched in the preceeding discussion of "The Dead." An alternative view of the autobiographical implications of *Dubliners'* form, presented in detail by Joseph Garrison, argues that the sequence of narrators reflects Joyce's gradual movement toward a more objective perspective. In "The Sisters," the narrator is bewildered by his vision of "the grey face" that "desired to confess something." Highly appropriate to the boy's confusion, Joyce's first-person style, according to Garrison, reflects a subjective perspective inimical to true art. By the end of "Grace," however, the narrative voice is much calmer, able to reflect with comic equanimity on the absurdities of the scrambled public discourse. Seeking a position of true artistic objectivity, Joyce insinuates himself only indirectly into his book. By the end of "The Dead," according to Garrison, Joyce has embraced T. S. Eliot's credo: "Poetry is not a turning loose of emotion, but an escape from emotion, it is not the expression of personality, but an escape from personality." From this perspective. Joyce's obsession with himself as artist paradoxically results in a refined sense of writing that effaces the limited and limiting presence of the self.

JOYCE AS CATHOLIC MORALIST

Whatever their focus, most autobiographical approaches imply that *Dubliners* is *about* writing and/or writers. The resulting emphasis on the relationship between narrative voice, character, and author creates a somewhat solipsistic Joyce obsessed with his own problems. Although this image closely resembles the "biographical" Joyce, it provides relatively little help in understanding his solutions to these problems. Providing support both for Garrison's image of Joyce as objective observer and for my own image of Joyce as sympathetic participant, the autobiographical approach invites readers to accept Joyce's self-valuation, including his reticences and limitations. Such a narrowed vision, however, obscures crucial aspects of the mature Joycean sensibility. The imagination that created *Dubliners* is not purely aesthetic; it is also moral, involving values as well as techniques. Grounded in Joyce's education, these essentially Catholic values permeate *Dubliners* from its specific imagery to its encompassing vision of human failure and fulfillment.

On the most obvious level, Joyce was deeply influenced by the Catholic educational system. Observing the "caretaker" presence of the Jesuit Order at University College, Kevin Sullivan's exhaustive study *Joyce Among the Jesuits* stresses the impact of the *Ratio Studiorum,* the plan of study followed in Joyce's early education at Belvedere. Sullivan quotes the Jesuit General Luis Martin's comments on the *Ratio* as follows: "The characteristics of the Ratio Studiorum are not to be sought in the subject matter, nor in the order and succession in which the different branches are taught, but rather in what may be called the 'form,' or spirit of the system. This form, or spirit, consists chiefly in the training of the mind, which is the object, and in the various exercises, which are the means of attaining the object." Where the exercises developed specific powers of reasoning and analysis, the training of the mind assumed central importance. Basing their plan of education on general moral and religious principles, the Jesuits, for the most part, were relatively unconcerned with propagating specific points of dogma. Throughout his life, Joyce maintained his respect for both the intellectual rigor and the interest in underlying processes and principles embedded in the *Ratio Studiorum.* His interest in systematic philosophy, reflected in the aesthetic theory he derived primarily from St. Thomas Aquinus, testifies to the deep impact of his Jesuit training.

However deeply embedded in his sensibility, Joyce's Catholicism should not be understood in institutional terms. In *Dubliners,* it takes more subtle, and perhaps more basic, forms. To be sure, the book includes a multitude of allusions to Catholicism. If Ireland is a priest-ridden race—as John Joyce informed his son—then *Dubliners* is an appropriately priest-ridden book. The absence of priests in a particular story is more noteworthy than their presence. While many references fulfill primarily realistic functions, others embody elements of parody and social commentary. For example, Joyce based the commercially minded Father Purdon in "Grace" on Father Bernard Vaughan, whose flashy performing style combined with his opportunistic theology to elevate him into a distinctly unpriestly public prominence during the early 1900s.

Throughout *Dubliners,* Joyce's treatment of symbolic detail assumes a certain degree of familiarity with Catholicism. The effectiveness of the reference to the Blessed Mary Margaret Alacoque in "Eveline" relies on the knowledge that, in theory, adhering to the Order of the Sacred Heart assures domestic peace. Similarly, Father Flynn's disorientation in "The Sisters" assumes meaning only in relation to the theological implications of the broken chalice, which holds the host during communion. Although in strict theological terms, Father Flynn has committed no sin, his response indicates that he may be haunted by the thought that he has spilled the blood of Christ. Even more disconcerting, Father Flynn may take the absence of external consequences as an indication that no transformation of the host has taken place, that the communion is merely an empty social ritual, that his vocation is a delusion. Whatever the theological position invoked, any comprehensive interpretation of Father Flynn's paralysis—which provides an organizing image for *Dubliners* as a whole—must incorporate an awareness of the specifically Catholic framework.

At times, Joyce manipulates Catholic materials in an extremely intricate manner, as in the hilarious discussion of papal "mottos" and the doctrine of infallibility in "Grace." Discussing Pope Leo XIII, whom he calls "one of the great lights of the age," Martin Cunningham cites the appropriateness of his motto: *"Lux upon Lux— Light upon Light."* When Mr. Fogarty counters that the motto was actually *"Lux in Tenebris . . . Light in Darkness"*—amended by M'Coy to *Tenebrae*—Mr. Cunningham insists that his version is correct. Referring to Leo XIII's support of secular scholarship, Cunningham contrasts him with his predecessor Pius IX: "his predecessor's motto was *Crux upon Crux*, that is, *Cross upon Cross*—to show the difference between their two pontificates." The next sentence reads: "The inference was allowed." As Richard Adams observes in *Surface and Symbol:* "Both disputants are wrong on the main point at issue; yet between them they have something roughly like the right idea. The first motto has something to do with crosses, and the second with light. They were wrong, in passing, on a further point, for popes do not 'take mottoes.' What they are talking about is the so-called 'Prophecies of Malachias,' in which the Irish saint foretold, in a phrase apiece, the characters of the popes to come." The actual mottos, as Adams discovered, were *"Crux de Cruce"* and *"Lumen in Coelo."* Underlying his parody with the transformation of an obscure theological detail, Joyce implicitly critiques the lax democratic approach to matters of theological doctrine and factual detail. Particularly in the context of the discussion of infallibility, the parody takes on an additional dimension. If the Dubliners are incapable of accuracy even in regard to historically verifiable facts—they misquote Dryden's "Great wits are sure to madness near allied," inaccurately declare "Dowling" (actually Dollinger) a member of the College of Cardinals, etc.—how can they hope to comprehend spiritual mysteries?

Beyond such specific allusions, which Joyce puts to a variety of uses, Catholicism permeates the underlying imagery and structure of *Dubliners*. In his influential study "The Unity of *Dubliners*," Brewster Ghiselin concludes that the book's unity "is realized, finally, in terms of religious images and ideas, most of them distinctively Christian. . . . The unifying action may be conceived of . . . as a movement of the human soul, in desire of life, through various conditions of Christian virtue and stages of deadly sin, toward or away from the font and the altar and all the gifts of the two chief sacraments provided for its salvation." Indeed, *Dubliners* abounds with images of frustrated communion, from Father Flynn's broken chalice in "The Sisters" through the Christmas season dinner, notably lacking in references to Christ, in "The Dead." Detailing his argument, Ghiselin identifies a systematic analysis of the three theological virtues, the four cardinal virtues, and the seven deadly sins in *Dubliners*. The youthful protagonists of the first three stories attempt to live with faith (in Father Flynn), hope (of escape and adventure), and love (for Mangan's sister), only to find their impulses frustrated by their paralyzed environment. Similarly, Eveline fails to summon the virtue of fortitude, thus ensuring her entrapment. Subsequent stories demonstrate the impact of the sins of pride (Jimmy Doyle's sense of himself as a cosmopolitan playboy); covetousness (Lenehan and Corley's desire for the servant girl's money); lust (the sexual intrigue leading to Doran's entrapment in marriage); envy (Chandler's feeling toward Gallaher); anger (Farrington's mistreatment of his child); gluttony (the focus on Maria's gift of the plumcake); and sloth (Duffy's inability to break out of his solipsism). Several critics extend this essentially allegorical approach, providing convincing support for Ghiselin's thesis. Virginia Moseley's *Joyce and the Bible* catalogs references to numerous Catholic sacraments and rituals. Reiterating and revising Ghiselin's focus on the seven deadly sins, Mary Reynolds identifies specific parallels between individual stories and the cantos of Dante's *Inferno*. Despite his alienation from the Catholic Church, Joyce continued to judge his characters from a perspective grounded in the moral norms of the Catholic tradition.

Both the concern with specific theological concepts and the structural importance of religious narratives have long been recognized as central elements of "Grace," a crucial story for any Catholic interpretation of *Dubliners*. Building on the title image—which in Catholicism refers to an unmerited gift from God that enables the recipient to resist temptation and perform good works—several critics view the story as an allegory of salvation. Joseph Baker and Father Robert Boyle have developed elaborate allegorical readings that cast Kernan in the role of fallen man. For Baker, Power represents God the Father; Cunningham represents God the Son; M'Coy represents the Holy Ghost; the "sandy-haired chap" represents Satan; and Fogarty represents St. John. Boyle's more elaborate reading provides the following identifications: the Cyclist/Christ; Constable/the Old Testament Law; Bar Manager/Moses, Satan; Two Gentleman/Father and Holy Spirit; Mrs. Kernan/Irish Catholicism; Cunningham/High Church Anglicanism; Power/Low Church Anglicanism, etc. Somewhat less ambitious in his project, F. X. Newman interprets the story as a reworking of the tale of Job with Kernan in the role of Job. In the three sections of "Grace," Joyce presents Job's fall (the accident), his encounter with the comforters (the visit from Cunningham and company), and the voice of the Lord from the whirlwind (Father Purdon's sermon). While most religiously inclined critics accept Newman's analysis, Stanislaus Joyce's identification of the parallel with the *Divine Comedy* has attracted more enthusiastic support, particularly in Reynold's definitive study.

Each of the three sections represents a book of the *Comedy:* described in terms of darkness and filth, the scene in the lavatory is clearly infernal; the visits mark Kernan's passage through the healing purgatory; Father Purdon's sermon is an ironic vision of paradise. Preparing for the parodic conclusion that quite obviously contrasts commercial salvation with the beatific vision of the *Paradisio,* Joyce bases his treatment of the characters in "Grace" specifically on Dante's condemnation of the flatterers, who wallow in excrement in the eighth circle of hell. When the story opens, Kernan lies in his own filth in the washroom. As the story progresses, characters continually flatter one another in preparation for the climactic flattery of Father Purdon's sermon.

Originally intended as the conclusion of *Dubliners,* the final passage of "Grace" can be read either as vicious condemnation or a statement of comic equanimity. In accord with the Uncle Charles Principle, the narrative voice assumes the tones of the simoniac priest who willingly confuses monetary and spiritual values:

> Jesus Christ was not a hard taskmaster. He understood our little failings, understood the weakness of our poor fallen nature, understood the temptations of this life. We might have had, we all had from time to time, our temptations: we might have, we all had, our failings. But one thing only, he said, he would ask of his hearers. And that was: to be straight and manly with God. If their accounts tallied in every point to say:
>
> —Well, I have verified my accounts. I find all well.
>
> But if, as might happen, there were some discrepancies, to admit the truth, to be frank and say like a man:
>
> —Well, I have looked into my accounts. I find this wrong and this wrong. But, with God's grace, I will rectify this and this. I will set right my accounts.

By ending the story with this baldly flattering passage, which in effect denies the reality of sin and/or paralysis, Joyce undercuts Father Purdon and his listeners. The effectiveness of the passage rests on the unstated norm provided by an uncorrupted, implicitly Catholic, conception of grace. While the theological framework remains implicit, as it does in most of the stories of *Dubliners,* it is nonetheless vital to an understanding of Joyce's sensibility.

Extending both the general theological framework and the specific Dantean parallel, Father Boyle has developed a four-level exegesis of "Grace." Employing the categories suggested by Dante for analysis of the *Divine Comedy,* Boyle explores literal, moral, allegorical, and anagogical levels of meaning in the story. The literal level, which concerns Kernan's progress from the bar to the church, expresses Joyce's condemnation of Kernan's paralyzed moral sensibility. On the moral level, Joyce traces the movement from Dublin secularism (Kernan in the bar) to Dublin Christianity (Kernan in the church). Still essentially parodic, this level of meaning emphasizes the failure of Dublin religion to provide an adequate source of, or channel for, true spiritual impulses. Informing each of these levels, however, Father Boyle finds an intricate pattern of implied values that give meaning to the parodies on the lower levels. On the allegorical level, Joyce traces the movement from the Old Testament through various sectarian interpretations of the New Testament—reflected in the confusion over church doctrine— to the final Communion of the Saints and Vision of the Truth. Closely paralleling the allegorical level, the anagogical level moves from the general condition of original sin through baptism and the unmerited gift of grace (the invitation to the retreat) to the closing vision of God.

Beneath his contempt for the fallen, paralyzed state of religion in Dublin, then, Joyce intimates, through structure and image, a belief in the possibility of virtue and salvation, without which the satire takes on a cynical, nihilistic undertone. By no means dogmatic, a strongly moral vision informs *Dubliners.* In assessing the overall relevance of Joyce's Catholicism to this moral vision, the Dantean parallel is very much to the point. Rather than directly identifying the center of value—the moral norm represented by the virtues in their uncorrupted form—Joyce arrives at the norm through Dante, another exile who combined social satire with theological seriousness. Reflecting the Jesuit training that instilled a respect for authority and subtlety of rhetorical strategy, Joyce arrives at his surprisingly orthodox vision in a characteristically indirect manner. It is important not to oversimplify the meaning of God's love. As Father Boyle argues, for Joyce God's love entails the expansive sympathy of an actual grace that maintains validity as a moral ideal, however remote from the daily experience of the Dubliners living in a city defined by its paralyzed priests.

JOYCE AS SYMBOLIC MYTHOLOGIST

While no critic disputes the presence of Catholic elements in *Dubliners,* some see Joyce's use of Christianity not as an endorsement, but as one aspect of a more extensive concern with the relationship between "myth" and experience. T. S. Eliot provided the classic statement on Joyce's use of myth, which he accorded the importance of a scientific discovery. For Eliot, Joyce's use of a "continuous parallel between contemporaneity and antiquity" provides "a way of controlling, of ordering, of giving a shape and significance" to contemporary life. Although Eliot was responding primarily to *Ulysses,* Joyce had begun experimenting with mythic parallels in *Dubliners,* which he originally planned to title *Ulysses in Dublin.* Usually discussed in relation to the myths of classical antiquity, Eliot's definition can be applied to the use of any preexisting framework—any material (story, image, character) that encodes an established understanding of experience—juxtaposed with contemporary events. Although Eliot (in keeping with his own perspective) argues that Joyce uses this parallel to emphasize "the immense panorama of futility and anarchy which is contemporary history," the juxtaposition can be used for many different purposes. Invoking a parallel between Gabriel Conroy and his angelic namesake could most certainly be a satirical gesture emphasizing the distance separating the Dublin journalist from divine wisdom. Seen from a slightly different perspective, however, it could alert the reader to spiritual aspects of Gabriel's character that might otherwise be overlooked.

The importance of recognizing the larger mythic framework of Joyce's references to Catholicism can be seen in the analysis of a seemingly minor character in "Grace." When Kernan is discovered in the lavatory, a "young man in a cycling-suit" emerges from the crowd gathered around him. The young man calls for water, washes the blood from Kernan's mouth, and offers him brandy. After Kernan revives, the young man asks "You're all right now?" before receding into the background. From Father Boyle's Catholic perspective, the young man represents Christ, who through his sacramental cleansing bestows the grace enabling fallen man to rise up from his stupor. From a mythological perspective, this understanding is not so much inaccurate as incomplete. Focusing on the precise description of the young man's clothing suggests a second level of mythic identification. Whereas the Catholic view of fall and salvation assumes progress from "lower" to "higher" states, the invocation of "cycles" suggests the nonlinear approach to myth that Joyce derived from Giambattista Vico's philosophy of history. Joyce's understanding of Vico centered on the cyclic movement from Divine Age through Heroic Age to Human Age. Following a "ricorso," a period of regeneration, the cycle begins again. By the time he employed Vico's cycles as a central structural element in *Finnegans Wake,* Joyce had developed an elaborate set of correspondences (linguistic, political, psychological) for each age. In *Dubliners,* no such correspondences exist. Rather, Joyce uses Vico—the young man in the cycling suit—to introduce an alternative view of Kernan's "resurrection." From the cyclic perspective, the Christian vocabulary of fall and redemption is simply one way of expressing the universal rhythm of decline and rebirth. To the extent that it offers escape from cyclic repetition, an exclusively Christian vocabulary oversimplifies what Joyce presents as an inherent rhythm of human experience.

The coexistence of Christ and Vico in a single image highlights a crucial aspect of Joyce's use of myth, one that obviates the necessity of "choosing" between the linear and cyclic readings of resurrection. Joyce frequently offers multiple mythic frameworks for understanding a single event. Resisting the simplifications inherent in any one mythic system, this highlights Joyce's complex treatment of the relationship between myth and psychology. Although they live in accord with a variety of religious and/or political myths, most characters in *Dubliners* are only dimly aware of the implications of the beliefs. As a result, they are unable to see beyond the limits of their particular frameworks. Frequently, Joyce alludes to myths that are entirely unknown to his characters, suggesting alternatives to the limits they unquestioningly accept. While Cunningham, Power, and Kernan believe in a Catholic myth of linear salvation, from a Viconian perspective that belief reflects a dangerous naivety that dooms them to repeated, and unconscious, "falls into history."

Employing images appropriate to specific characters, Joyce alludes to diverse myths for local effect without attempting to impose a unified structure. In "Araby" the "wild garden behind the house" contains "a central apple-tree," clearly suggesting the tree of knowledge in the Garden of Eden. Perhaps the "rusty bicycle-pump" symbolizes the serpent. However detailed the correspondences, invoking the Christian myth of the fall expands the significance of the boy's disillusionment. Not simply an individual disappointment, his knowledge of the world's corruption, revealed in the conversation between the young men and the salesgirl, is as old as Adam and Eve. Joyce employs non-Christian myths in a similar manner. The musician playing the lament "Silent, O Moyle" in "Two Gallants" takes on a larger significance through his association with the harp, the traditional symbol of Ireland: "His harp too, heedless that her coverings had fallen about her knees, seemed weary alike of the eyes of strangers and of her master's hands." Joyce links the victimization of the individual Dubliner with the victimization of Ireland, to which he contributes by dragging its mythic emblem into the streets for "the eyes of strangers." The references to the "wild west" in "An Encounter," the medieval theory of "humors" in "A Painful Case," and the "Three Graces" in "The Dead" suggest mythic meanings similar to those in "Araby" and "Two Gallants."

In addition to such local meanings, Joyce occasionally employs myth as the central aspect of a story. For example, he intertwines a number of mythic elements to provide a wider perspective and raise disquieting questions concerning Maria, the central character of

"Clay." Set on Halloween, "Clay" exploits various mythic elements to underscore Maria's isolation. Described as a Halloween witch—"she had a very long nose and a very long chin"—Maria seems one of the lost souls who wander the night before All Soul's Day. Numerous details emphasize this mythic identity, most notably her choice of the clay, emblem of death, in the fortune-telling game. On one level, then, Joyce uses the mythic parallel in a straight-forward manner to portray the painful isolation of an unattractive woman in Dublin. Of equal significance, however, is Joyce's awareness of the myth's larger relevance to Dublin society. Reflecting Maria's limited insight into her own situation, "Clay" is written in an extremely simple, almost child-like style that represses potentially unpleasant perceptions or experiences. Characters repeatedly taunt Maria about her unmarried state: Lizzie Fleming teases her that she will get the ring (emblem of marriage) in the fortune-telling game; the clerk in the bakery asks her if she is buying a wedding cake. In each case, Maria reacts with laughter, as if the teasing is harmless. No one mentions that she has omitted the verse dealing with marriage from "I Dreamt that I Dwelt." Maria never acknowledges the degree of her isolation, her status as a lost soul. The self-consciously cheery language—"He was very nice with her"; "soon they were all quite merry again," etc.—fails to mask the painful fact that the best fate anyone can imagine for Maria is that she might enter a nunnery, symbolized by the prayer book that is substituted for the clay. Substituting a Catholic myth for the harsher—and probably more accurate—myth suggested by the clay, the Dubliners participate in Maria's self-deception. Emphasizing their refusal to acknowledge realities, Joyce hints that they are all lost souls, condemned to reenact the myths they repress.

Individual consciousness of mythic relationships is not necessary, or even necessarily desirable. For Maria, self-consciousness might do nothing but enforce a sense of despair. One common approach to myth in *Dubliners* focuses on elements that are entirely inaccessible to Joyce's characters. Taking their cue from the abandoned title *Ulysses in Dublin,* Charles Shattuck and Richard Levin constructed an elaborate argument that Joyce modelled each of the stories in *Dubliners* on material drawn from the first half of the *Odyssey*. The first three stories suggest parallels between the young narrators and Telemachus, a fatherless boy who undertakes several quests; the stories of adolescence are associated with Odysseus' difficult journey home; the stories of maturity with the tales he tells to Alcinous. Perhaps because Joyce had begun to envision a subtler use of the materials in *Ulysses*, the Homeric parallels are less extensive or central in the stories of public life. Applied to particular stories, the Homeric parallel in *Dubliners* functions ironically, emphasizing the distance between Joyce's characters and their heroic analogs. Based loosely on the "Nausicaa" episode, "Two Gallants" echoes numerous elements of the original story. Corley's relationship with the slavey, who wears the sailor's colors of blue and white, parallels Odysseus' romance with the daughter of a sailor-king. Sharing Odysseus' strength and his willingness to recount his adventures, Corley plays Odysseus to Lenehan's Alcinous. Like Odysseus, Corley conceals his name from the girl, who nonetheless, like Nausicaa, recognizes his nobility, his "bit of class." Even the Irish harpist has a Homeric antecedent in Demodocus, a blind harpist. As in most of the stories in *Dubliners,* according to Shattuck and Levin, these parallels emphasize the failure of Corley and Lenehan to achieve the nobility of their mythic predecessors.

Although parallels with Homer can be extracted from every story in *Dubliners*, many—particularly those concerned with plot—may point not to specific literary debts, but to deeper structures uniting seemingly disparate mythological systems. Emphasizing the similarities between heroic stories from numerous cultures, this approach has been codified in Joseph Campbell's conception of the "monomyth." Campbell, who was fascinated by Joyce's later books, identifies a cyclic pattern in which a hero of obscure parentage, with the aid of mysterious helpers, answers a call to adventure. Undergoing a series of trials, the hero (usually through a descent to the underworld) attains a "boon" (usually gold, which is associated with psychic or spiritual wholeness). Surviving another sequence of trials, the hero completes the cycle by returning home to bestow the boon upon his community, an act frequently symbolized through marriage. From this perspective, both the *Odyssey* and the story of Jesus are simply variations on a more basic mythic structure. The fact that patterns present in these sources recur in *Dubliners* may attest to the archetypal quality of Joyce's imagination. "Araby," which, like many of the later stories Joyce wrote, is particularly dense in mythic references, certainly attests to this archetypal quality. Drawing on the mythic association of the east with rebirth—reflected both in the Catholic tradition of building churches with their head to the east and in the beliefs of numerous cults celebrating the rising sun—Joyce sends his nameless hero on a journey across Dublin to a mythic "Araby," associated with spiritual rebirth, sexual love, and release from the paralysis of Irish culture. Similar eastward movements recur frequently in the first half of *Dubliners;* the boys in "An Encounter" follow an eastward course across Dublin; Eveline considers escaping to the eastern sea; Little Chandler associates freedom with the "Oriental eyes" of Jewish women. The absence or attenuation of such mythic impulses in the last half of the book attests to the progressive destruction of even the most basic spiritual impulses.

This shattering of Campbell's archetypal pattern highlights a crucial aspect of Joyce's use of myth in *Dubliners.* Using the "monomyth" not as determining pattern but as a basis for comparing particular manifestations emphasizes the ways in which a given text differs from the basic pattern. Viewed from this perspective, two aspects of *Dubliners* stand out, both suggesting that the archetypal patterns exist in Dublin only in the trivialized forms appropriate to Vico's human age. First, Joyce fragments the quest, replacing the mythic hero with a composite "Dubliner." Second, no fragment of the quest is successfully completed. The failure of the hopeful individual quests in "An Encounter" and "Araby" leads inexorably to the wholesale abandonment of the questing impulse and, by extension, of the hope of human fulfillment. In the later stories, the predominant movement is either westward (toward the mythic land of death) or circular (reflecting both the underlying cyclic pattern and the actuality of cultural disorientation). It would be possible to soften this portrait in a number of ways. First, it could be argued that the presence of cyclic patterns in the work suggests the coming of a ricorso, a period of regeneration.

If Kernan's resurrection is not to be understood as proof of his ultimate salvation, neither is it evidence of ultimate damnation. Alternatively, a morally inclined critic could create a reading of "The Dead" arguing that Joyce uses mythic elements to support the theme of redemption. (Chapter 6 of this study provides just such a reading.) In relation to *Dubliners* as a whole, however, such "positive" interpretations are only marginally convincing. Joyce's consistent emphasis on the limitations of individual characters and of Irish culture generally suggests the accuracy, for *Dubliners* as well as *Ulysses*, of Eliot's contention that myth serves Joyce primarily as a means of emphasizing the "anarchy and futility" of contemporary experience.

JOYCE AS SOCIOHISTORICAL REALIST

Even as Joyce shaped the intricate symbolic structures of *Dubliners*, he remained aware that extraliterary realities inevitably influenced, and on occasion forced redefinition of, symbolic meanings. By no means so abstract a book as philosophically or aesthetically inclined critics sometimes imply, *Dubliners* recognizes that history establishes constraints on imaginative freedom. Combining his awareness of history, environmental forces, and individual consciousness, Joyce's polished realism incorporates unusually complex perceptions into what remains an essentially realistic, representative form. The fact that he employs techniques not usually associated with realism—mythic parallels, complicated allusions, multileveled narrative voices—reflects Joyce's refusal to accept the unnecessary limitations associated with realistic conventions rather than an underlying dissatisfaction with the realistic impulse.

Discussing the meaning of "realism" for Joyce's contemporaries, George Becker identifies three basic criteria: verisimilitude; an emphasis on the representative rather than the exceptional (both in plot and character); and an objective, rather than idealistic, view of human nature and experience. Judged in terms of these criteria, *Dubliners* is clearly a realistic book. Based to a large extent on actual people, places, and events, the stories present an easily recognizable world in a relatively "undistorted" manner. The use of characters from all socioeconomic levels—from the un- or underemployed Lenehan in "Two Gallants" through the affluent Morkans in "The Dead"—reflects Joyce's desire, codified in the book's plan, to provide a truly representative picture of Dublin. Although it would not be precisely accurate to call Joyce's attitude "objective," his view of characters such as Farrington in "The Boarding House" or Corley in "Two Gallants" is certainly not "idealistic." Examining the interaction between psychology, environment, and action, Joyce's emphasis on subjective experience is motivated by his desire to express reality in its full complexity, rather than a transcendent conception of human nature.

Approaching one element of this complexity in a technically innovative manner, Joyce employs subtle allusions to suggest the impact of history on his characters, whether or not they are conscious of particular events or patterns. Characteristic of Joyce's approach, "Two Gallants" derives its meaning in large part from its historically resonant settings. As Donald Torchiana has demonstrated, Lenehan and Corley walk past a sequence of places—among them the Kildare Street Club and the Rotunda Hospital—associated with the oppressive Protestant Ascendency. Although neither shows even a glimmer of historical awareness, Joyce suggests that their aimlessness originates in the English dominance that has cast Dublin into a permanent economic depression. Unable to find satisfactory work, the young men dissipate their energies by exploiting others, particularly women, for trivial monetary gain. The scene with the harpist typifies Joyce's use of setting to suggest unrecognized, but extremely significant, historical contexts. Emphasizing the multifaceted degradation of Ireland, the scene takes place in front of the Kildare Street Club, a haven of Unionism, which Joyce viewed as a political manifestation of Irish self-betrayal. Entirely unaware of the historical origins of their actions, Corley and Lenehan's ignorance dooms them, and Ireland, to perpetuate patterns that, as long as they remain unconscious, severely limit their socioeconomic possibilities.

As it did for many nineteenth- or early twentieth-century novelists, Joyce's realism at times brought him into conflict with public moral standards, particularly in relation to his controversial treatment of sexuality. Determined not to exclude any aspect of reality, particularly one central to understanding many types of behavior, Joyce deals directly with issues such as homosexuality ("An Encounter") and the use of sexuality for financial gain ("Two Gallants," "The Boarding House"). Similarly, Joyce insisted on using the actual language spoken on the Dublin streets, including the conventionally proscribed curse "bloody": "she brought me two bloody fine cigars" in "Two Gallants"; "he'd bloody well put his teeth down his throat" in "The Boarding House"; and, the most controversial use because of its reference to the English royal family, "Here's this fellow come to the throne after his bloody owl' mother keeping him out of it till the man was grey" in "Ivy Day in the Committee Room." Not surprisingly this frankness generated a good deal of resistance, particularly from the editors and printers who were afraid such material would be found obscene in court. Joyce's commitment to a realistic aesthetic was deep enough that he continued to insist on the verisimilitude of his portrait, even though it contributed to the long delay in publication of *Dubliners*.

Although such a defense of controversial material could be mounted for purely practical reasons—to speed publication—it is in fact difficult to isolate any titillating or sensationalistic passages in *Dubliners*. Perhaps the most daring of the stories in regard to content, "An Encounter" raises issues of homosexuality, sadomasochism, and, at least indirectly, child molestation. Yet Joyce focuses not on the details of the old man's behavior, but on the boy's fascination and response. After the old man comments that "Every boy . . . has a little sweetheart," the narrator evaluates this "strangely liberal" attitude: "In my heart I thought that what he said about boys and sweethearts was reasonable." When the old man goes on to describe his feelings about young girls, the narrator focuses on the manner of speech rather than the implicitly sexual content: "He began to speak to us about girls, saying what nice soft hair they had and how soft their hands were and how all girls were not so good as they seemed to be if one only knew. There was nothing he liked, he said, so much as looking at a nice young girl, at her nice white hands and her beautiful soft hair. He gave me the impression that he was repeating something which he had learned by heart or that, magnetized by some words of his own speech, his mind was slowly circling round and round in the same orbit." When the man leaves the two boys, probably to masturbate, Joyce's description is far from sensationalistic, consisting simply of Mahony's exclamations "I say! Look what he's doing!" and "I say . . . He's a queer old josser!" Even when the old man returns to spin his more directly threatening sadomasochistic fantasies, the narrator continues to focus on his voice: "He described to me how he would whip such a boy as if he were unfolding some elaborate mystery. He would love that, he said, better than anything in this world; and his voice, as he led me monotonously through the mystery, grew almost affectionate and seemed to plead with me that I should understand him." Throughout the final scene of "An Encounter," Joyce seems primarily interested in the impact of sexuality on psychology, rather than sexual perversion as such. Particularly when juxtaposed with the references to the boys' escapist reading—wild west stories from boys' magazines such as *The Union Jack, Pluck,* and *The Halfpenny Marvel;* the romantic novels of Walter Scott—Joyce seems to be suggesting that the failure to acknowledge aspects of reality renders individuals susceptible to the fascination of the taboo, the unknown. Playing on the narrator's repressions, the old man implicates the youth in one aspect of the Dublin paralysis. From this perspective, the frankness of "An Encounter"—a matter of psychology as much as sexuality—resists the very corruption it was accused of furthering.

A closely related set of issues concerns Joyce's portrayal of women. At first glance, the women in *Dubliners* seem to have been consigned to stereotypical roles: Mangan's sister in "Araby" resembles the unattainable virgin; Polly Mooney's manipulative sexuality in "The Boarding House" identifies her as a temptress/whore; Maria in "Clay" is a stereotypical old maid; Little Chandler's wife treats her husband like an infant; Mrs. Kearney is a conventionally domineering mother in "A Mother." Yet, as Florence Walzl demonstrates, Joyce grounds his presentation of women in the observed facts of Dublin life. The women in *Dubliners* work at the full range of jobs typically available to women at the time. They run boarding houses (Mrs. Mooney), teach music (Mary Jane and Aunt Kate in "The Dead"), work as accompanists (Kathleen in "A Mother"), or servants (Lily in "The Dead," the slavey in "Two Gallants"). In addition, Joyce's portrait of the teacher Molly Ivors, who more than holds her own with Gabriel Conroy, both intellectually and socially, admits the possibility of exceptional women capable of asserting themselves against immense environmental pressure. Like the reluctant feminist Henrik Ibsen, who exerted a major impact on Joyce's attraction to realistic forms, Joyce hints that, beneath their circumscribed roles, women possess untapped potential.

The accuracy, centrality (half the stories of the adolescence and maturity sections have female protagonists), and range in Joyce's presentation of women suggest a revised understanding of their stereotypical qualities. Recognizing the limitations inherent in Irish life, Joyce presents their implications in a realistic way. Just as Corley and Lenehan unconsciously enact roles shaped by their environment, Joyce's women, living in a society that circumscribes the possibilities of all but an extraordinary few, assume the roles with which they are familiar. In an economic context that casts most Dubliners, male or female, into some degree of poverty, family life suffers from severe distortions. Delaying marriage because they are unable to support families, young men such as Corley and Lenehan come to view sexuality as an adventure or a source of financial gain. Responding in kind, Mrs. Mooney and Polly simply employ the resources at their disposal to acquire some measure of security. Men conditioned to spend their time primarily with other men—the expedition of "An Encounter" recurring in the camaraderie of "After the Race," the wandering of "Two Gallants," and the backroom banter of "Ivy Day in the Committee Room"—have no way of communicating with their wives once they do marry. As a result, characters such as Farrington in "Counterparts" and Little Chandler in "A Little Cloud" seek out male companionship, leaving their wives at home. Lacking meaningful contact with their husbands, the women pour energy into their children. The result is the stereotypical, but realistic, attitude of Little

Chandler's wife who showers her infant with a smothering affection that initiates a new cycle of sexual alienation: "My little man! My little mannie! Was 'ou frightened, love? . . . There now, love! There now! . . . Lambabaun! Mamma's little lamb of the world! . . . There now!" There seems little chance that Chandler's son will negotiate the path to maturity any more effectively than has his father. Forced to break the maternal bond to attain any sense of independent selfhood, he will almost inevitably perceive women—themselves trapped in the same set of forces—as forces attempting to shut him away from the world of male companionship.

This is not to suggest that the Joyce of *Dubliners* should be seen as a feminist. Neither his temperament nor his aesthetic encouraged such a stance. Perhaps the strongest pressure on a realistic aesthetic comes from ideological sources that seek to interpret the meaning of events in relation to particular patterns of interpretation. At least potentially, such ideological pressure implies the exclusion of material, however seemingly trivial, that might contradict the ideology. For Joyce, this amounts to little more than an attempt to reestablish the censorship basic to the repressions that paralyze the men and women of Dublin. Resisting ideology as another form of convention, Joyce insists on the complexity of the reality he sees.

A DECONSTRUCTIVE DREAM OF JOYCE

But let us interrogate the text. The problem with these readings—not just those calling themselves "realistic"—is that they imply a simple relationship between "words" and "reality." For authority they invoke "James Joyce," "the narrator," "Gabriel Conroy," "Father Flynn," "Lily": subjects whose "reality" remains unquestioned. But the text of *Dubliners* casts these premises into doubt. In the curiously titled "Counterparts"—the reader is implicated as silent counterpart in a whispered dialogue on the nature of our oppositions, our divisions, and our absences—a group of words, not a completed sentence, intimates what elsewhere, for fear of paralysis—the end of writing—cannot be said:

> "*In no case shall the said Bernard Bodley be . . .*"

The ellipsis is present in the text. (The quotation marks—"Joyce" hated inverted commas—have been added.) An awareness, mediated, distanced, emerges through "Farrington," paralyzed by his inscription of nonexistence: "He took up his pen and dipped it in the ink but he continued to stare stupidly at the last words he had written: *In no case shall the said Bernard Bodley be . . .*"

The text embarrasses itself, interrogates its own reality. *In no case shall.* There is no configuration of forces, no possible state of being capable of contradicting what has been inscribed. The future is revealed as blank. What *shall* happen in a world defined through negation? Possibilities, illusions, recede from the field of vision. And with them, subjects: *the said Bernard Bodley.* Who, what, is "Bernard Bodley"? Words on a page. Who, what, is "Farrington?" Words on a page. No different from Bernard Bodley, his double in nonexistence. Or not quite his double. Bernard Bodley has been "said." The text bears a trace of something other, a lost state where the name has been joined with voice, with the living breath of a subject who cannot be contained, translated, inscribed. (And the living breath, the communion of humanity and the divine in a vital community: that, too, an absence, not even a memory in the fragments of the human age, the ruined myths of departed gods, "Parnell" resurrected in a poem that is recited, repeatedly *said.* Sharing the malaise, the Dubliners lend "Farrington," like "Parnell," a simulacrum of life through repeated *retellings* of his tale.) Still, removed from the breath of life, ossified in writing, Bernard Bodley no longer is. There is *no case* that shall allow him to *be.* Never having been said, Farrington shares only the absence of Bernard Bodley—his counterpart as written sign—not his lost presence. Devoid of existence, Farrington (for economic purposes) spends his time writing, copying the words of others, words that confront him with the stark separation of writing and the other world:

In no case shall the said Bernard Bodley be . . .

This avoids, as the central anxiety of this text (the book *you* are reading). As insubstantially linguistic as "Farrington," "Joyce," if he exists at all, exists only in defracted, dispersed form, like the mono-mythic hero of *Dubliners.* Invoked by critics in the manner of the Hebrews addressing their refractory, uncooperative, and nameless Lord, the Joycean "self" leaves traces of its finally unimaginable being throughout the text, which represents, in this allegory, the world created by the divine breath. But this "self" assumes meaning in relation to its very absence, its coexistence with a "real" "self" that, worst of all, is "somewhere else." "Joyce" questions all of this in that single sentence, *In no case shall the said Bernard Bodley be . . .,* which, literally (as Lily the caretaker's daughter was run off her feet) redefines everything else in the text. That single moment of awareness subjects every word in *Dubliners* to radical revision.

And it cannot be overemphasized that this does not preclude talking about the "world." Rather, it suggests a new way of doing so, a process predicated on the raising of an unasked question, the resurrection of the dead:

In no case shall the said Bernard Bodley be . . .

And this represents only one case. The anxiety over word/reality, presence/absence pervades *Dubliners.* The first paragraph of "The Sisters" comes to rest, as revised, on the distance between words and world: *paralysis, gnomon, simony.* "I" knows the words' power; acknowledges them as avatars of authorities strong enough to claim singularity: *the* euclid, *the* catechism. (The addition of italics—Bernard

Bodley's nonexistence exists only in italics—alters the significance of the claim. Bringing existence out of nonexistence, the reader/critic assumes the role of the God of the moment.) In the consciousness of the text—a consciousness ascribed to a young boy still capable of claiming his subjective "I"—signifiers (the words used) relate to signifieds (the objects to which they refer) through discrepancy. From this tension: *signs*. Not neutral language, not reality, the *sign* encodes a tension, lends (or enforces) meaning, provides a means of talking / writing / thinking about a world more various than the sign can say. So the sign cannot say the world. To articulate is to exclude. And one point of "deconstruction"—one possible sign for the process we have been carrying on in this section—is to acknowledge the process and the exclusions, the limitations of the world of words:

In no case shall the said Bernard Bodley be . . .

And if a "real Joyce" can be traced through *Dubliners*, it emerges as much from what is repressed as from what is articulated. The repressions emerge in glimmers, nodes, repeated complexes of associated images that reveal the separate "stories" as arbitrary markers, attempts to attribute recurring obsessions to "others," "characters" like "Gabriel Conroy," "Farrington," or the suspiciously multiple "I"s. It is possible to dream toward the absent center of *Dubliners*. Fritz Senn and Hélène Cixous have done so, although their decision to begin at the beginning—each dreams out of "The Sisters"—reflects a curious bondage to the logical structure imposed by the linear form of the book. Recurring images, the nodes of half-repressed images that hint structure throughout the Joycean texts (the divisions between *Dubliners, Ulysses, Finnegans Wake* as conventional as those between "Clay," "Ivy Day in the Committee Room," "A Mother," "Grace," "The Dead"). Recurring images: the woman in half-light, inspiring the sexual desire of "Araby" or "The Dead"; the primal punishment of father and son refracted through "An Encounter" and "Counterparts," the punishment of reader by text and text by reader revealed as the present counterpart of the memory encoded in Farrington and the son he cannot even name:

—Who are you? Charlie?
—No, pa. Tom.

This from a "Joyce" who, in all jocoseriousness, could not remember how many sisters he had. Farrington's brutality, his own rage over the encompassing loss of communion, potency, name.

In no case shall the said Bernard Bodley be . . .

And, despite the absence of the body in the dream, this is not to speak Freud. Because, like the Catholic God (of whom we have spoken with Father Boyle) and Marx (of whom we shall speak anon), Freud inscribes a discourse of the Father. Oedipus—Farrington, John Joyce, the James Joyce who fathered a son as *Dubliners* was being written— organizes the world, provides a center, enforces meaning. Through coercion, inevitably (by directing the construction of the sign, always a result of unnecessary choices). Through violence, if need be. But the energies of the text, calling their own authority into question, resist. "Joyce's" words plunge us into a field of play, a field of language supporting alien processes alongside the familiar. Still "jung and easily freudened," the "Joyce" of "*Dubliners*" envisions escape from the inscriptions of paternal anxiety. Feminine energy escapes containment. "Molly Ivors" leaves the party. Marginalized, her absence—the absence of the feminine—is double. She cannot remain with the dead, with Gabriel Conroy and Bernard Bodley. Or even with "Lily," a sign for the inquisition of the patriarchs, "all palaver and what they can get out of you." Uncontained by "palaver," uncontainable, "Molly Ivors" reminds us of a different process, an unnamed, un- (though not anti-, the negation implying the center) patriarchal field of play beyond the words of any text.

In no case shall the said Bernard Bodley be . . .

And behind all, behind the escape of the feminine: the anxiety of the dream, the encompassing absence, the everlasting things that must not be said. The silence of the ellipsis, the whiteness of the page that gives shape to the letters of words that structure the world. Things that must not, that cannot, be said, leaving us to contemplate the silence of the Dublin that was Beckett's as well as Joyce's, filled with whispers hinting God or Self or Meaning. . . .

In no case shall the said Bernard Bodley be . . .

Despite appearances, all this is not to no point. Nor is it centrally important. A critical approach such as that employed in this section raises questions, heightens certain kinds of awareness. To repeat, it does *not* preclude, or even limit, other types of discussion. Potentially, it can enrich them. Even as early as *Dubliners*, Joyce—and having established the contingency and ambiguity of such terms, it seems unnecessary to belabor it further—seems to have been aware of the philosophical paradoxes inherent in the writing process. Rather than withdrawing into a purely intellectual contemplation of paradox, however, Joyce's treatment of Farrington suggests that failure to confront the void behind the conventions of daily life may have serious implications. Unwillingly, Farrington confronts the ambiguity of his own existence: he feels himself to be as insubstantial as Bernard Bodley, whom he inadvertently transforms into Bernard Bernard, a "mistake" that simply reaffirms Farrington's sense of the arbitrariness of human identity. He has had a brief glimpse through a hole in the conventional fabric of life, a fabric woven to cover up the emptiness at the center of being. (To digress one final time: perhaps Farrington represents humanity's first glimpse past the reassuring solidity of the Newtonian worldview into the relativistic field of play, toward the neutron stars that swallow up all light, toward the quantum emptiness of the subatomic depths, the flickering—from a human perspective— energy of the quarks that appear, here as in *Finnegans Wake* (which provided physicists with the word "quark") although, as yet, without name.

Reduced to brutishness by his perception of nonbeing, Farrington first attempts to reestablish self-hood by incessantly retelling the tale of his triumph. But palaver and alcohol, the rituals of patriarchy, provide no escape. (Molly Ivors is far away, in spirit and in text.) So Farrington—the vengeful father of the rebellious young Joycean dream—beats his son. Unable to process his experience—either social or psychological—Farrington surrenders his humanity. Grounding his most abstract philosophical passages in his most brutally naturalistic plot, Joyce reminds us that abstraction can be another form of evasion, that "reality"—however indefinable—remains. *Dubliners* does not belabor its deconstructive implications. One sentence can be enough: *In no case shall the said Bernard Bodley be . . .* Farrington is not. Joyce is not. Craig Werner is not. But we continue to engage the text, as we continue to engage the world. "Counterparts" suggests that we engage the world with a fuller knowledge of the ambiguities of our process, with an acceptance of an undefinable void: the source of our freedom, the expansive ground of our process. Unremembered, the void turns to a terror that makes of us, as of "Farrington," brutes.

RECONSTRUCTING A POLITICAL JOYCE

Responding to the academic emphasis on the aesthetic intricacy and philosophical ambiguity of modernist literature, Afro-American critic Michael Thelwell writes:

> What is absolutely clear is that the emergence and rise of modernism in Europe represented a rather abrupt turning away from what had been the first responsibility of the novelist—that of *communicating* generally shared and accessible truth and perceptions, which implicitly must mean socially and culturally derived insights and knowledge. In the celebration of the individual consciousness, communication became secondary to "self-expression," no matter how arcane, private, and neurotic its inspiration. Similarly, the emphasis on literary allusion (cannibalism), elaborate structural invention, and private reference as ends in themselves is obviously not geared

primarily to communication. James Joyce, a celebrated pioneer down these literary cul-de-sacs, is alleged to have boasted that only four people fully understood *Finnegans Wake* and that two of them were dead. While the story may be apocryphal, the reverence in the voice of the teacher who told it to me was not—and that is significant. It was also said of Joyce, by no means the worst offender among the modernists, that it used to be that novelists were men of wide learning and broad interests in human events. What Joyce demonstrated was that all a novelist needed to know was himself.

Thelwell's position is significant not so much for what it says about Joyce as for what it says about what Joyce has come to mean. For Thelwell, as for a great many politically active readers, Joyce's work cannot be separated from the implicitly reactionary institutional settings where it is most frequently discussed. Whatever political message he might have intended, Joyce shows little interest in communicating with an audience outside a literary elite, implicitly perpetuating the values of a decadent culture in which art has lost its active relationship to political life. Applied to *Dubliners,* such an approach sees the text itself as another symptom of the encompassing paralysis. Joyce's retreat to individualism and aestheticism—a defining tendency of mainstream Anglo-American modernism—typifies the bourgeois withdrawal from the world. Perceiving the world through the false consciousness propagated by the British oppressors, Joyce and his Irish compatriots are incapable of even imagining the possibility of political action.

A number of distinct responses can be made to such criticism. The simplest is to acknowledge the accuracy of the critique, admitting that the significance of *Dubliners* is primarily aesthetic, that even at the outset of his career Joyce considered himself above political concerns that would have compromised his objective contemplation of human behavior. The political exhaustion pervading "Ivy Day in the Committee Room" reflects Joyce's own disillusionment, his belief that all political activity flounders on the inadequacies of human nature. Parnell's significance, from this perspective, lies primarily in his mythological identity with the betrayed hero of the monomyth (or with

Christ) rather than his position as a nationalist leader struggling against British oppression. From this perspective, political life provides material for aesthetic reflection; the text serves no more active purpose.

A second response to Thelwell's criticism perceives a more active political potential in *Dubliners*. Written before Joyce had embraced the high modernist aesthetic of *Ulysses* and *Finnegans Wake*, *Dubliners* provides a textual field that admits the possibility of a truly political literature. Several stories intimate the political dimension of Joyce's work. "After the Race," for example, includes a suggestive subtext linking Irish and Hungarian politics. As Zack Bowen observes, Joyce included the Hungarian Villona in the card party in part as an allusion to Sinn Fein leader Arthur Griffith's political pamphlet *The Resurrection of Hungary*, originally published in the *United Irishman*. Drawing a parallel between the oppression of Hungary and that of Ireland, Griffith recommended adaptation of the Hungarian nationalist's refusal to accept the suspension of the Hungarian constitution, a strategy that would reinstate the Constitution of 1792 as the law of Ireland. Contrasting the relatively capable Villona with the ineffectual Jimmy Doyle, Joyce suggests that the Irish psychological paralysis is grounded in the absence of an adequate political strategy.

Not all of the political implications of *Dubliners* are so arcane. As the story most directly concerned with political issues, "Ivy Day in the Committee Room" brings into focus a number of profound issues regarding the status and potential of the political text in the real world. Resisting the academic tendency, quite rightly condemned by Thelwell, to separate literature from its contexts, *Dubliners* encourages readers who have not excluded political considerations to reconsider the nature of political meaning in a literary work of another place or time. Beyond the explicit politics of an author or text—which take on a secondary importance—this approach focuses attention on the ways in which political "meaning" relies on context, either historical or contemporary. An exploration of the original context of "Ivy Day in the Committee Room" draws attention to the political tensions at work within Ireland in the late nineteenth and early twentieth centuries,

thereby providing insight into a particular stage of historical development. A clear analysis of the problems of the Irish nationalist movement casts light on potential problems within similar movements in
other contexts. An emphasis on the contemporary context—the circumstances in which the story is *read*—raises related political issues.
For a reader (particularly a nonacademic reader) without access to (or
interest in) the details of Irish politics, the political statements made
by characters in "Ivy Day in the Committee Room" assume meaning
primarily in relationship to the contemporary status of ongoing ideological debates. While the concept of "nationalism" may have provided an outlet for political resistance in Joyce's day, its significance
has changed substantially as a result of intervening historical events.
From this perspective, any interpretation of "Ivy Day in the Committee Room" assumes significance in an ongoing struggle for control of
the political discourse that shapes the real world.

As a first step toward understanding "Ivy Day in the Committee
Room" in relation to its original historical context, it is useful to examine Joyce's professed political beliefs. During the period when he
was writing *Dubliners*, Joyce frequently identified himself as a socialist. Commenting on his "socialist tendencies," Joyce wrote to the skep-
tical Stanislaus: "Can you not see plainly from facts like these that a
deferment of the emancipation of the proletariat, a reaction to cleri-
calism or aristocracy or bourgeoisism would mean a revulsion to tyr-
annies of all kinds. . . . For my part I believe that to establish the
church in full power again in Europe would mean a renewal of the
Inquisition."[27] As this statement implies, Joyce saw socialism more as
an alternative to Church power than as a means of transforming economic and political relationships. When juxtaposed with Joyce's deep
feelings concerning Parnell, it seems clear that the roots, and perhaps
the substance, of his socialism lay somewhat paradoxically in the Irish
Nationalist movement, which maintained a distinctly capitalist perspective. As Malcolm Brown observes, Parnellism was a "gut issue,"
rather than an intellectual political philosophy, in the Joyce household.
Both the novelist and his father blamed the collapse of Parnell's movement primarily on the priests who denounced him from the pulpit

following the public revelation in 1889 of his affair with Kitty O'Shea. Joyce's first poem, "Et Tu, Healy," written when he was nine years old and subsequently distributed by his father, was a satirical attack on Timothy Healy, a Parnell lieutenant who proved instrumental in his political defeat. The abandonment of Parnell by many of his followers and the subsequent failure of the Home Rule movement during the 1890s soured Joyce on nationalism. Yet his life-long identification with Parnell, combined with the vague generalities of his socialist statements, suggest that Joyce's politics retained a strong nationalist undercurrent.

When read with an awareness of its historical context, "Ivy Day in the Committee Room" can be seen as Joyce's critique of, and lament over, the collapse of nationalism. Far from a romantic portrait of a remembered movement, the story emphasizes that the attenuation of active political impulses, the trivialization of political discourse, reinforces the oppression against which Parnell struggled. Joyce constructs "Ivy Day in the Committee Room" around the contrast between the absent leader Parnell and the Dubliners whose cynical attitudes dishonor his memory. As any contemporary Dubliner would have known, "Ivy Day" is 6 October, the anniversary of Parnell's death, on which his followers wore sprigs of ivy in commemoration. Similarly, the term "committee room"—an allusion to Committee Room 15 where the vote to remove Parnell from leadership of the Home Rule movement was held—would have alerted Joyce's contemporaries to the theme of betrayal. Set in the early 1900s—Joyce based the story on his brother Stanislaus's experiences of 1902—the story centers on the total exhaustion that had set in since Parnell's death. The "Nationalist" candidate Richard Tierney, like Parnell a leader who never actually appears in the story, offers no outlet for political energy. Identified on his campaign card as a "P.L.G." (Poor Law Guardian), a position widely identified with the oppression of the poor, Tierney poses no threat to entrenched English interests. Seeking the support of Conservative voters following the withdrawal of their candidate from the election, Crofton dismisses nationalism as a tangential issue, going so far as to emphasize Tierney's stake in the status quo: *"He's a big rate-payer. . . . He has extensive house property in the city and three places of business and isn't it to his own advantage to keep down the rates? He's a prominent and respected citizen . . . and a Poor Law Guardian, and he doesn't belong to any party, good, bad, or indifferent."* The corruption of Parnell's commitment to the liberation of Ireland could not be more baldly presented.

Against this pervasive backdrop of corruption, Joyce presents a gallery of political malaise. None of the Nationalist workers shows any interest in anything other than getting paid. None evinces even a wistful hope that the political system offers any hope for change. As Florence Walzl observes, each of the characters who visits the committee room highlights a different aspect of the malaise. Author of the poem on Parnell's martyrdom, Hynes invokes the fallen leader in the discussion of Edward VII's planned visit: "If this man was alive, he said, pointing to the leaf, we'd have no talk of an address of welcome." But even Hynes's nationalism is suspect; after he leaves, Henchy accuses him, through innuendo, of being a British agent, "in the pay of the Castle." As middleman for Tierney, Henchy seems totally unconcerned with the blatant lack of respect shown his candidate by his ostensible supporters. The slightly disreputable Father Keon represents the clergy who helped drive Parnell to his death. Crofton, the former Conservative canvasser, makes not even the slightest pretence of supporting any nationalist position. Perhaps the most damning portrait in Joyce's gallery of Dublin politics, however, is the boy from Tierney's pub, who comes alive only when he is offered a drink. However grimy the present of Dublin politics, its future appears no brighter.

Both the image patterns and allusions underscore the theme of paralysis. Old Jack's desultory attempts to start a fire at the beginning of the story simply highlight the cold and damp. Joyce's use of Anatole France's "The Procurator of Judea" as a model for "Ivy Day in the Committee Room" draws attention to the political dimension of the analogy between Christ and Parnell. In France's story, Pontius Pilate recalls his experience in Judea but, when questioned, cannot even remember Jesus of Nazareth's name. From the standpoint of the existing political system, the heroic figure signifies nothing. The following exchange, the first actual mention of Parnell in the story he dominates, casts the canvassers in the role of Pilate:

—But look here, John, said Mr. O'Connor. Why should we welcome the King of England? Didn't Parnell himself . . .
—Parnell, said Mr. Henchy, is dead.

The entire discussion of Edward VII's visit reiterates the loss of political vitality. Although O'Connor assures his listeners that Tierney will not vote in favor of an address of welcome for the British monarch on his trip to Ireland, Hynes clearly distrusts the Nationalist candidate: "Wait till you see whether he will or not. I know him. Is it Tricky Dicky Tierney?" Even more damning, Henchy defends Edward against Lyons's implied charge of moral corruption:

—But after all now, said Mr. Lyons argumentatively, King Edward's life, you know, is not the very . . .
—Let bygones be bygones, said Mr. Henchy. I admire the man personally. He's just an ordinary knockabout like you and me. He's fond of his glass of grog and he's a bit of a rake, perhaps, and he's a good sportsman. Damn it, can't we Irish play fair?

When Mr. Lyons reiterates his position, Henchy refuses to entertain the discussion: "where's the analogy between the two cases?" Joyce felt no further need to underscore the irony of this talk of fair play for the philandering English king from the political heirs of a leader driven from power because of an affair with a woman he ultimately married.

The reading of, and response to, Hynes's poem "The Death of Parnell" provides a fitting climax. Self-consciously "poetic" in image and rhythm, the poem celebrates Parnell as Ireland's "Uncrowned King," culminating in the hope that he will "Rise, like the Phoenix from the flames," thus ushering in "The day that brings us Freedom's reign." Despite the accusation that he works for the British, Hynes is the one character in the story who seems to remember what Parnell stood for; most critics have judged his poem to be sincere, if uninspired. Although the Dubliners gathered in the Committee Room respond to the reading first with silence, then with applause, and finally by drinking, it seems clear that, even in an explicitly political setting on Ivy Day, Parnell no longer possesses the power to unify or inspire. Their political energy dissipated, the Dubliners have no way of responding to a poem that even implicitly demands action. In order to defuse the tension, Henchy turns to Crofton, who as a Conservative, would be the least likely person to share Hynes's emotions:

> —What do you think of that, Crofton? cried Mr. Henchy. Isn't that fine? What?
> Mr. Crofton said that it was a very fine piece of writing.

The poem is anything but fine writing. Its strength lies in the sincerity of its impulse, its refusal to forget in a context characterized by collective amnesia. Focusing on the writing enables Crofton, and the rest of Hynes's audience, to avoid the poem's uncomfortable political implications. Curiously anticipating the main thrust of Thelwell's criticism of "elite modernism," Joyce presents technical criticism as an evasion of all that, in a living political culture, the poem might mean.

In part because it can be approximated only through research and laborious reconstruction, the meaning the story might have had for Joyce's contemporaries has lost much of its power. This does not, however, deprive "Ivy Day in the Committee Room" of all political significance. Rather, it relocates that significance in the ways the text handles political issues that continue to command attention. Reading the story in light of subsequent political developments, the contemporary reader can achieve a clearer vision both of the limitations Joyce shares with the Dubliners and of the ways he intimates alternatives not available to them. Applied to "Ivy Day in the Committee Room," such an admittedly revisionist reading process reiterates and extends Joyce's dissatisfaction with nationalism. Although they were just beginning to emerge as Joyce wrote, the subsequent difficulties of nationalistic movements from Nazi Germany to sub-Saharan Africa strongly suggest that the problems Joyce describes result from contradictions inherent in bourgeois nationalism, not from its betrayal.

"Ivy Day in the Committee Room" contains a surprising amount of evidence that Joyce sensed these contradictions. Recalling Falstaff's fantasy of becoming king in Shakespeare's *Henry IV,* Joyce parodies the aspirations of the Dubliners. Unable to conceive of an alternative to the corruption around them, they envision power in terms of personal indulgence and patronage. Henchy assumes the role of City Father, "driving out of the Mansion House . . . in all my vermin, with Jack here standing up behind me in a powdered wig, eh?" Among the "vermin"—the Lord Mayor of Dublin wore ermine—will be O'Connor, who immediately volunteers for the role of private secretary and Father Keon, who will be appointed private chaplain. Joyce makes it clear that the Dubliners think of power not as a means of alleviating shared problems but as a path to indulgence and domination of others. They are unable to understand why the current Lord Mayor might want to eat pork chops, roundly condemning his lack of style.

The false consciousness that leads the canvassers to identify their own aspirations with those of their oppressors is created in part by a narrow nationalism that fails to address underlying economic issues. Again, Joyce seems at least dimly aware of the economic dimension of the problem in his treatment of Crofton and Henchy. As might be expected of a Conservative, Crofton's support of Tierney centers on his status as a man of property and his willingness to enforce the Poor Laws. Nationalism as such presents no alternative to economic exploitation. Even more extreme as a comment on nationalism, Henchy associates his acceptance of the British oppressor directly with his capitalist values: "What we want in this country, as I said to old Ward, is capital. The King's coming here will mean an influx of money into this country. The citizens of Dublin will benefit by it. Look at all the factories down by the quays there, idle! Look at all the money there is in the country if we only worked the old industries, the mills, the shipbuilding yards and factories. It's capital we want." Nothing indicates Henchy or Tierney's willingness to address the exploitative implications of reopening the factories under English domination. Grounded in their commitment to the capitalist values that have reduced their country to destitution, their desire for power precludes any form of political action, based on either nation or class, that might alter the underlying economic organization. Only Hynes expresses a serious critique of the value structure when he says "The working-man . . . gets all kicks and no halfpence. But it's labour produces everything. The working-man is not looking for fat jobs for his sons and nephews and cousins. The working-man is not going to drag the honour of Dublin in the mud to please a German monarch." Henchy's innuendo against Hynes, from this perspective, is revealed as an attempt to defuse an attack on the economic interests that, though not articulated, provide the core of the nationalist ideology.

Recognizing the elements of the text that suggest the contradictions in the nationalist value structure does not, of course, prove that Joyce was a sophisticated Marxist thinker. His dislike of Crofton and Henchy centers on their betrayal of Parnell, only secondarily involving their bourgeois aspirations. Parnell's nationalism provided the young Joyce with his strongest image of constructive political action. To some extent, as a man of his era, he remained locked in an ideology that had collapsed by the time he reached his maturity. Nevertheless, "Ivy Day in the Committee Room" raises issues of continuing relevance in an era when cynicism and false consciousness have become increasingly prevalent. Despite his limitations, Joyce hints at a truly liberating vision. Emerging in distorted, fragmentary forms, his political insights draw attention to issues—of power and freedom—that cannot be resolved within a purely textual reality. Like Bertolt Brecht, a modernist who saw no contradiction between technical experimentation and political commitment, Joyce provides raw material for the political analysis that must precede action. Read today, without the preconceptions reflected in Thelwell's criticism, *Dubliners* encourages its readers to become more aware of the limits of their own discourse, and challenges the paralyzing complacency that accepts the world as given.

· 8 ·

"A LITTLE CLOUD" AND JOYCE'S DEMOCRACY OF CONSCIOUSNESS

To reduce Joyce to proto-Marxist, post-Catholic, or proto-deconstructionist is to preclude possibilities. To accept tensions—the apparent contradictions of the constructions presented in the preceeding chapter—is to enter a Joycean world more complex than any described by a single explanatory system. The implications of such acceptance are not abstract. Not simply an intellectual exercise, the way any given reader combines approaches determines the potential significance and uses of a particular text in a particular context. The remainder of this chapter presents one particular engagement with "A Little Cloud," one of the last stories Joyce wrote for *Dubliners*. In "processing" the story, which has received surprisingly little critical attention other than an insightful reading by Father Boyle, I will be testing the hypothesis—which may well be revised in the course of the engagement—that "A Little Cloud" is Joyce's strongest statement in support of what I call the "democracy of consciousness." As I have throughout this study, I will work on the assumption that a critical approach that omits or simplifies other approaches reflects the limitations of the critic rather than the author, text, or audience. Grounded in this assumption, my hypothesis reflects my commitment to certain values: a populist politics that assumes the equal value of each human being; a populist aesthetic that assumes an active political role for art in the real world; and a modernist aesthetic that assumes the desirability of articulating the full complexity of experience, even when that complexity calls other values into question. While Joyce would probably have differed with aspects of the first two positions, there is sufficient evidence to indicate that, in *Dubliners,* he was still concerned, at least indirectly, with the possibility of communicating a complex vision to a general audience. As his early interest in cinema and his later, obsessive championing of the Irish singer John Sullivan indicate, Joyce maintained an interest in popular art forms. His friends were not always members of any literary or intellectual elite. Most important, his treatment of "average"—which, from a populist position, is to say exceptional—characters such as Little Chandler repudiates the major premise of elitist condescension. While Chandler could not have written "A Little Cloud," the style of the story would not exclude him from its audience. To recognize Chandler's limitations is not necessarily to understand the quality of his life. Unless we are willing to impose a limiting perspective on Chandler's experience, the best way to comprehend Joyce's presentation is to enter into the flow of the story without simplification and with as few preconceptions as possible. Armed with access to various approaches to and sources of information concerning *Dubliners,* we can now begin to process "A Little Cloud," to constitute a meaning from the text.

The story's title, which alludes to Dante's *Inferno,* alerts us to several levels of possible meaning. As Mary Reynolds observes, Dante's phrase "si come nuvoletta" describes the flame hiding Ulysses and the other false counselors. Shortly, it will become apparent that Joyce is alluding not to Tommy Chandler, but to Ignatius Gallaher, whom he describes "emerging after some time from the clouds of smoke in which he had taken refuge." Immediately, however, the allusion serves primarily to underscore the theme of betrayal and to activate Catholic and/or mythological approaches to the text.

Introducing one of the major motifs of the story, the first paragraph focuses on the tension between Chandler, the Dubliner who has remained in Ireland, and the glamorous exile Gallaher. Embodying the Uncle Charles Principle, the paragraph is suffused with Chandler's admiration for Gallaher, whose name evokes Ignatius Loyola, the founder of the Jesuit order, whom, as Father Boyle notes, Joyce associated with cunning. Morally ambiguous, this cunning can be understood either as the protective element of Joyce's credo—"silence, exile, and cunning"—or as an aspect of the corrupt power of the Catholic Church. In the early stages of the story, however, power is primarily associated not with the church, but with English rule. Working in "the King's Inns," Chandler apprehends the image of "the great city London" as a mark of Gallaher's superiority. Internalizing the idea of his own inadequacy, an inadequacy directly associated with Dublin, Chandler acts in a self-demeaning manner: "he gave one the idea of being a little man."

Chandler's position in the economic system contributes directly to his acceptance of paralysis. Contrasting "his tiresome writing" with Gallaher's "brilliant figure on the London Press," Chandler feels exiled from life. Trapped in his office, he can only watch "the moving figures" outside as they move through the "gardens" that invoke a state of innocence from which Chandler feels exiled. Repressing both his personal jealousy and the political implications of his situation, Chandler resigns himself to paralysis: "He felt how useless it was to struggle against fortune, this being the burden of wisdom which the ages had bequeathed to him." In addition to characterizing Chandler, this sentence cautions against accepting "paralysis" as an unavoidable condition. Presenting Chandler's attitude as a mark of his resignation, Joyce intimates a countervailing message in the "wisdom which the ages had bequeathed to him." Unable to tap such an alternative, however, Chandler feels alienated from "the books of poetry upon his shelves at home." Although he feels recurrent urges to communicate through art—"he had been tempted to take one down from the bookshelf and read out something to his wife"—he can do nothing more than repeat "lines to himself."

Leaving the workplace in which he is little more than a peasant, Chandler passes beneath the "feudal arch of the King's Inns." Immediately he encounters signs that his own oppressed condition is typical of Dublin under British rule. Recalling Charles Dickens's harsh portraits of industrial London, Joyce describes the "horde of grimy children [who] populated the street. They stood or ran in the roadway or crawled up the steps before the gaping doors or squatted like mice upon the thresholds." Only dimly aware of his victimization, Chandler cannot accept what he sees. He ignores both the children and the "gaunt spectral mansions," historically resonant emblems of the "old nobility of Dublin." Gallaher's choice of a meeting place reinforces Chandler's sense of cultural inferiority that extends to the waiters who "he had heard . . . spoke French and German." For Chandler, Corless's is an inaccessible realm occupied by "cultured" (i.e., economically privileged) women as idealized and inaccessible as the goddesses of Greek myth: "Their faces were powdered and they caught up their dresses, when they touched earth, like alarmed Atalantas."

To this point, Joyce's portrait emphasizes Chandler's paralysis, his repressions. The final two sentences of the sixth paragraph, however, introduce another aspect of his character: "Sometimes, however, he courted the causes of his fear. He chose the darkest and narrowest streets and, as he walked boldly forward, the silence that was spread about his footsteps troubled him, the wandering silent figures troubled him; and at times a sound of low fugitive laughter made him tremble like a leaf." Juxtaposed with Joyce's image of himself as a silent, alienated wanderer on the streets of Dublin, this passage associates Chandler with the figure of the modernist artist. Anticipated in his alienation from commercial writing, Chandler's apprehension of "the silence" framing his movement attests to a level of awareness that receives no encouragement in his daily life. With no way of expressing or processing such near-epiphanies, Chandler represses their implications. Yet Chandler remains ill at ease with conventional language. Thinking over Gallaher's "greatness," Chandler momentarily senses the inadequacy of the language that reinforces his paralysis. Unable to remember concrete evidence of Gallaher's "future greatness," Chandler falters: "There was always a certain . . . something in Ignatius Gallaher that impressed you in spite of yourself." The ellipsis draws attention to the gap between signifier and signified, language and reality.

Having established Chandler's character and circumstances, Joyce turns his attention to an aspect of Chandler's character with direct autobiographical significance. Signalled by the phrase "that was one version of his flight," Joyce—who had already begun to identify his artistic exile with the winged flight of Stephen Dedalus—projected alternate versions of his own character onto Chandler and Gallaher. Inspired by fantasies of his friend's success, Chandler envisions himself, and the world, in terms recalling the attitude of the young Joyce who, armed with a clear feeling of his own worth, departed from Dublin shortly after he started to express its encompassing paralysis. Feeling "himself superior to the people he passed," Chandler's "soul revolted against the dull inelegance of Capel Street." Dismissing the potential of his native land, he sees exile as the only viable alternative open to the would-be artist: "There was no doubt about it: if you wanted to succeed you had to go away. You could do nothing in Dublin." Like the Joyce who began to contrive his own artistic mythology even before he had published a book, Chandler envisions his future triumphs in detail. He will write poems characterized by "a melancholy tempered by recurrences of faith and resignation and simple joy." To assure a positive response from the English critics, he resolves to "put in allusions." Coming from the most allusive of modern novelists—who frequently added specific allusions in the process of revision—this cannot be dismissed as simple parody. Nor can his question: "Could he write something original?" Joyce certainly provides his readers with the opportunity to condescend to Chandler, to dismiss him as a pathetic self-deluded clerk. Such a response, however, is immediately called into question by Joyce's presentation of the condescending Gallaher. Trapped in "his own sober inartistic life," Chandler embodies Joyce's fears concerning what might have happened to him if he had remained in Dublin. As a second fantasy-Joyce—the talented Irishman who succeeds in the cultured capital—Gallaher presents an even more sobering image. Associated with the dull colors that throughout *Dubliners* are emblems of paralysis, Gallaher is no more vital than Chandler, who he always addresses in the diminutive "Tommy." Gallaher's heavy drinking, which has not changed since his departure eight years earlier, emphasizes his similarity to the aimless friends, such as "Poor O'Hara," he has ostensibly surpassed.

Throughout his conversation with Chandler, Gallaher assumes a condescending attitude. Dismissing Chandler's trip to the Isle of Man, he celebrates the vitality of Paris: "it's the life of Paris; that's the thing. Ah, there's no city like Paris for gaiety, movement, excitement. . . ." (Joyce's ellipses). Given Gallaher's London residence, the fact that he associates vitality with Paris suggests an alienation as deep as that of Chandler when he looks out at the garden. Despite a vague uneasiness—he perceives "something vulgar in his friend which he had not observed before"—Chandler continues to envy Gallaher. Gallaher reciprocates by reiterating his condescension. Declaring that Paris is "not for a pious chap like you," Gallaher dismisses Chandler's questions about the immorality of Paris with "a catholic gesture." Already associated with British oppression, Gallaher's gesture implicates him in the corruption of religious life. Unwilling to entertain questions of morality, Gallaher makes no attempt to distinguish between beauty and corruption. A parodic compression of mythological figures, Gallaher combines the roles of Atalanta, who was forced to choose between her suitors, and Paris, forced to choose the most beautiful of goddesses. After summarizing the vices of the Continent, Gallaher "seemed inclined to award the palm to Berlin," an inclination again reflecting his tendency to project vitality into exotic settings separate from his own life.

At no point does Joyce present any real foundation for Gallaher's sense of superiority. Suggesting uncomfortable parallels with readers who assume a condescending attitude toward Chandler, Joyce subverts Gallaher's stature. Not content with his own achievements, which are never specified in the story, Gallaher bolsters his self-image by diminishing Chandler. Encouraging him to drink to excess, Gallaher furthers Chandler's surrender to self-pity and paralysis. As his refusal of the dinner invitation demonstrates, Gallaher has little real interest in Chandler. Nothing in Gallaher's attitude suggests that he has any intention of honoring his pledge to accept an invitation on his next visit to Dublin. Gallaher's willingness to seal the promise with another drink amounts to little more than one more in the sequence of "false communions" that permeate *Dubliners*. A transparent attempt to deny his actual paralysis, Gallaher's vehement assertion of future sexual and financial potency only emphasizes their current absence: "I've only to say the word and to-morrow I can have the woman and the cash. . . . You wait a while, my boy. See if I don't play my cards properly. When I go about a thing I mean business, I tell you. You just wait." Unintentionally revealing his desire that Chandler remain paralyzed, this statement also associates Gallaher with the card-playing Irishman Jimmy Doyle. Juxtaposed with his condescending attitude, Gallaher's lack of actual achievement raises serious doubts about the intrinsic superiority of the exile (or the reader) over the victim, whose paralysis is only more obvious, not more profound.

The final section of "A Little Cloud" extends the implications of Chandler's meeting with Gallaher. Returning home, Chandler reenters a world where his lack of economic success—the roots of which he has refused to examine—plays a central role. Saddled with the duties of housekeeping and childrearing, Annie Chandler has internalized the pervasive sense of paralysis. Joyce's realistic depiction of her emotional exhaustion suggests that her "bad humour" and "short answers" are not atypical. Yet Chandler, who has not acted on his impulse to share his experience of poetry with her, senses his wife's frustration only dimly. Rather than thinking of her realistic situation, he retreats into romantic contemplation of the picture of her in a "pale blue summer blouse" he had given her. Even that memory circles back to the economic issue: "when she heard the price she threw the blouse on the table and said it was a regular swindle to charge ten and elevenpence for that." Chandler attempts to counter his distress by thinking of Annie's gradual acceptance of the gift; after trying it on, she "kissed him and said he was very good to think of her." But the hope of contact embedded in this image collapses. The next paragraph reads simply: "Hm! . . ." Again, the ellipses are Joyce's, pointing to the void behind the Chandler's fantasy/memory. Even this semiarticulate moment of perception is enough to force Chandler back to a harsher reality: "He looked coldly into the eyes of the photograph and they answered coldly." Given Chandler's socioeconomic and psychological paralysis, there seems little hope that he will be able to act on his fleeting vision of an escape from paralysis. In the context of his home, Chandler's creative impulses seem absurd even to himself. Reading Byron momentarily reawakens his desire to write: "Could he, too, write like that, express the melancholy of his soul in verse? There were so many things he wanted to describe." But after his infant son's crying breaks his reverie, he surrenders utterly to paralysis: "It was useless. He couldn't read. He couldn't do anything." Reiterating his unwillingness to confront the actualities of his own experience, Chandler breaks off in the middle (at the point marked *) of a stanza that reads in full:

> Within this narrow cell reclines her clay,
>> That clay where once* such animation beamed
> The King of Terrors seized her as his prey
> Not worth, nor beauty have her life redeemed.

Joyce contrasts this final moment of aesthetic feeling with the stark naturalism of the scene following Annie's return. Dismissing her husband with an all-too-familiar condescension, Annie reiterates the pattern of condescension in relation to her son. As Walzl has noted, this pattern has deep roots in the economic and sexual malaise of turn of the century Dublin. Alienated from their paralyzed husbands, Irish women shower a stifling affection on sons who will ultimately perpetuate the pattern of futile rebellion (expressed primarily through the empty rituals of the Dublin pubs), marital alienation, and maternal suffocation. Annie addresses the baby, who is never named in the text, as a "little mannie," "Mamma's little lamb of the world!" In a world without redemption, the allusions to Christ (the lamb of the world) seem particularly ironic.

Viewed by some critics as the central image of a redemptive epiphany, Chandler's "tears of remorse" have no apparent outlet in his life. If "A Little Cloud" offers any potential redemption—and I believe it does—that redemption lies primarily outside the text, in the adjustments of attitude suggested by Joyce's treatment of condescension. The roots of Chandler's paralysis lie in his internalization of Gallaher's and Annie's condescension (both of which have related sources). Condescending to himself, refusing to take his creative impulses seriously, Chandler limits himself to a pathetic role in the naturalistic psychodrama that ensures the continuing paralysis of his entire culture. Unable to conceive of alternative ways of thinking, his impulses are crushed. Yet the impulses are real, at least as real as those of Gallaher, the central image of condescension in the text. Attributing a number of his own perceptions to Chandler, Joyce seems aware that, had he remained in Dublin, his own impulses might have been crushed as Chandler's have been. The reader who accepts Gallaher's attitude, who claims a position of superiority over Chandler, in effect accepts a position in Dante's *Inferno*. Everyone, character or reader, who enforces paralysis, discourages alternatives, excludes the victims of paralysis from the democracy of consciousness shares the damnation. While the tears of remorse may not redeem Little Chandler, Joyce offers them to his readers as a cleansing epiphany, an inspiration to those determined to resist the spread of the intellectual and emotional paralysis that circumscribes our vision of human worth.

· 9 ·

THE PLURALITY OF INTERPRETATION AND THE MORAL OF *DUBLINERS*

Numerous versions of James Joyce circulate through this study: Joyce the autobiographer, Joyce the Catholic, Joyce the mythologist, Joyce the Realist, Joyce the reluctant feminist, Joyce the deconstructionist, Joyce the Irishman, Joyce the nationalist Marxist or Marxist nationalist, Joyce the modernist populist. Each of these images is contingent on a particular perspective, the acceptance of a set of premises—concerning literature and life—that are not, in any absolute sense, necessary. As a modernist text—a text that attempts to articulate extremes of subjective and objective attitudes—*Dubliners* provides a field for the exploration of various processes. As long as each process is viewed as contingent, partial, these processes need not be mutually exclusive. Juxtaposing one perspective with another, as we have done in the sequence of constructions, helps to highlight the material excluded or marginalized by each approach. Ideally, the sequence would be extended—it can never be completed—by subjecting the second approach to re-revision from the first perspective. Catholicism or deconstruction can cast light on the exclusions of Marxism and vice versa. Raising new questions, questioning the premises, is intended to help incorporate the widest possible range of insights into a particular processing of the book.

This plurality of interpretation returns us to Joyce's own vision of *Dubiners* as a study of paralysis. It should be emphasized that this pluralistic approach is itself grounded in a specific, and unnecessary, set of values: a populist approach to politics, a modernist commitment to complexity in aesthetics. Yet these values do not seem foreign to the Joyce of *Dubliners*. Again and again, Joyce presents characters imprisoned by their limited perspectives, their inability to see beyond the ways of processing reality offered by their immediate environment. The Dubliners *believe* in the reality, the necessity, of the systems in, and by, which they live. Yet Joyce makes it clear that the systems (religious, political, artistic, intellectual, sexual, economic) the Dubliners employ, whether consciously or not, to structure their lives in fact circumscribe reality and limit human potential. In this model of the world, to accept any given system is to invoke the "maleficent and sinful being," to further the "deadly work" of paralysis. Failing to question the world as given, the Dubliners paralyze themselves.

The greatness of *Dubliners* rests on Joyce's ability to implicate his readers in a situation analagous to that confronted by his characters, to challenge the complacency of the "objective" aesthetic observer. In some ways, Joyce's first book is even more complex than *Ulysses* or *Finnegans Wake* inasmuch as it is capable of supporting types of approaches excluded by the technical complexity of the later works that define (though not as tightly as is sometimes claimed) a particular *kind* of audience. Articulating the world in a way that might be accessible to the Dubliners themselves, Joyce maintains a vision of literature as an active form of resistance against paralysis. *Dubliners*, like Dublin, incorporates numerous versions of the world. To confuse any single version with the entire world—to deny the plurality of interpretation—is to paralyze: the text, the world, ourselves.

NOTES

1. Quoted in "Introduction: Modern Realism as a Literary Movement," in *Documents of Modern Literary Realism,* ed. George Becker (Princeton, N.J.: Princeton University Press, 1963), 166.

2. Ibid., 94.

3. *Letters of James Joyce,* vol. 2, ed. Richard Ellmann (New York: Viking Press, 1966), 122.

4. *Letters of James Joyce,* vol. 1, ed. Stuart Gilbert (New York: Viking Press, 1957), 63.

5. Ezra Pound, *Literary Essays* (Norfolk, Conn.: New Directions, n.d.), 402.

6. Edmund Wilson, *Axel's Castle* (New York: Scribner's, 1931), 191.

7. Harry Levin, *James Joyce* (Norfolk, Conn.: New Directions, 1960), 31.

8. David Daiches, *The Novel and the Modern World* (Chicago: University of Chicago Press, 1960), 84.

9. Robert Penn Warren and Cleanth Brooks, *Understanding Fiction* (New York: Appleton-Century-Crofts, 1959), 126.

10. T. S. Eliot, *Selected Prose of T. S. Eliot,* ed. Frank Kermode (New York: Harcourt Brace Jovanovich, 1975), 175.

11. Brewster Ghiselin, "The Unity of Joyce's *Dubliners,*" *Accent* 16 (Spring 1956): 83.

12. Ibid.

13. Homer Obed Brown, *James Joyce's Early Fiction: The Biography of a Form,* (Cleveland: Case Western Reserve University Press, 1978), 123.

141. Hélène Cixous, "Joyce: The (R)use of Writing," in *Post-Structuralist Joyce,* ed. Derek Attridge and Daniel Ferrer (New York: Cambridge University Press, 1984), 11.

15. Jean-Michel Rabaté, "Silence in *Dubliners,*" in *James Joyce: New Perspectives,* ed. Colin MacCabe (Bloomington: Indiana University Press, 1982), 23.

16. Colin MacCabe, *James Joyce and the Revolution of the Word* (London: Macmillan, 1978), 26.

17. John Paul Riquelme, *Teller and Tale in Joyce's Fiction: Oscillating Perspectives* (Baltimore: Johns Hopkins University Press, 1983), 73–74.

18. Ibid., 74.

19. *Letters,* 1:55.

20. Quoted in Ellmann, *James Joyce* (New York: Oxford University Press, 1982), 217.

21. *Letters,* 2:164.

22. *Letters,* 1:55.

23. Joyce's letter is quoted in Ellmann, *James Joyce,* 208.

24. *Letters,* 2:122.

25. Stanislaus Joyce, *My Brother's Keeper* (New York: Viking Press, 1958), 103–4.

26. Ellmann, *James Joyce,* 163.

27. *Letters,* 2:147.

BIBLIOGRAPHY

Primary Works

Dubliners, 1914. Reprinted, New York: Viking Press, 1961.

A Portrait of the Artist as a Young Man, 1916. Reprinted, New York: Viking Press, 1956.

Ulysses, 1922. Reprinted, New York: Random House, 1961.

Finnegans Wake. New York: Viking Press, 1939.

Stephen Hero. Norfolk, Conn.: New Directions, 1955.

Letters of James Joyce. Vol. 1 edited by Stuart Gilbert. New York: Viking Press, 1957. Vols. 2 and 3 edited by Richard Ellmann. New York: Viking Press, 1966.

Secondary Sources

Adams, Robert Martin. *Surface and Symbol: The Consistency of James Joyce's "Ulysses."* New York: Oxford University Press, 1962. Study focusing on *Ulysses*, which includes several suggestive statements concerning Joyce's balancing of symbolic and realistic perspectives.

ApRoberts, Robert P. "'Araby' and the Palimpsest of Criticism." *Antioch Review* 26 (Winter 1966–67):469–89. Rejoinder to Stone's essay on "Araby," reasserting a common-sense approach to the story.

Baker, Joseph. "The Trinity in Joyce's Grace,'" *James Joyce Quarterly* 2 (Summer 1965):299–303. Reads characters as allegorical representations.

Baker, Joseph, and Thomas Staley, eds. *James Joyce's "Dubliners": A Critical Handbook*. Belmont, Calif.: Wadsworth, 1969. Casebook including general essays and readings of particular stories.

Beck, Warren. *Joyce's "Dubliners": Substance, Vision, and Art.* Durham, N.C.: Duke University Press, 1975. Common-sense reading that resists nearly all symbolic meanings.

Becker, George, ed. "Introduction: Modern Realism as a Literary Movement." In *Documents of Modern Literary Realism,* 3–38. Princeton, N.J.: Princeton University Press, 1963. Summary of realistic movements in European and American literature including definitions of basic characteristics.

Beja, Morris, ed. *James Joyce, "Dubliners," and "A Portrait of the Artist as a Young Man."* London: Macmillan, 1973. Anthology of background materials, reviews and critical essays.

Benstock, Bernard, "Arabesques: Third Position of Concord." *James Joyce Quarterly* 5 (Fall 1967):30–39. Balances competing readings of Stone and ApRoberts.

———. *James Joyce: The Undiscover'd Country.* New York: Barnes & Noble, 1977. Emphasizes the tension between the Irish and the continental aspects of Joyce's temperament.

———. "The Dead." In *James Joyce's Dubliners: Critical Essays,* edited by Clive Hart. Emphasizes the importance of the epiphany season to the symbolic substructure of "The Dead."

———. "'The Sisters' and the Critics." *James Joyce Quarterly* 4 (Fall 1966):32–35. Attempts to develop a synthetic reading from previous antagonistic readings.

Bowen, Zack. "Hungarian Politics in 'After the Race,'" *James Joyce Quarterly* 7 (Winter 1970):138–39. Supplement to Bowen's essay in the Hart anthology, emphasizing parallels between Irish and Hungarian politics.

———. "Joyce and the Epiphany Concept: A New Approach." *Journal of Modern Literature* 9 (1981–82):103–14. Reconsideration of the epiphany, concluding that Joyce's use of the technique is more subjective than is usually recognized.

Bowen, Zack, and James Carens, eds. *A Companion to Joyce Studies.* Westport, Conn.: Greenwood Press, 1984. Excellent overview of Joyce studies including indispensable essay by Walzl summarizing readings of and approaches to *Dubliners.*

Boyle, Robert. "Swiftian Allegory and Dantean Parody in Joyce's 'Grace.'" *James Joyce Quarterly* 7 (Fall 1969):11–21. Elaborate reading of the multilevelled texture of "Grace," including a fully developed chart of the correspondences of anagogical, allegorical, moral, and literal meanings.

———. "'Two Gallants' and 'Ivy Day in the Committee Room.'" *James Joyce Quarterly* 1 (Fall 1963):100–106. Classic essay including analysis of the symbolic plot structure in "Two Gallants."

Bibliography

Brandabur, Edward. *A Scrupulous Meanness*. Urbana: University of Illinois Press, 1971. Study of Joyce's early work including a psychoanalytical reading of *Dubliners*.

Brown, Homer Obed. *James Joyce's Early Fiction: The Biography of a Form*. Cleveland: Case Western Reserve University Press, 1978. Insightful discussion of the shifting relationship between narrator and material, including a germinal discussion of "The Dead."

Brown, Malcolm. *The Politics of Irish Literature: From Thomas Davis to W. B. Yeats*. Seattle: University of Washington Press, 1972. Definitive discussion of the relationship between Irish literature and Irish politics with substantial emphasis on Joyce.

Campbell, Joseph. *Hero With a Thousand Faces*. Princeton, N.J.: Princeton University Press, 1968. Includes Campbell's influential discussion of the "monomyth."

Carrier, Warren. "*Dubliners:* Joyce's Dantean Vision." *Renascence* 17 (Summer 1965):211–15. Early statement of theme developed more fully by Father Boyle.

Chatman, Seymour. "Analgorithm." *James Joyce Quarterly* 18 (1981):293–99. Discusses attempts to apply his theoretical structure, developed in *Story and Discourse,* to *Dubliners*.

Cixous, Hélène. "Joyce: The (R)use of Writing." In *Post-Structuralist Joyce,* edited by Derek Attridge and Daniel Ferrer. New York: Cambridge University Press, 1984. Analysis of the first paragraph of "The Sisters," suggesting that Joyce's language casts the traditional conception of unified character into doubt.

Corrington, John William. "Isolation as Motif in 'A Painful Case.'" *James Joyce Quarterly* 3 (Spring 1966):182–191. Identifies "A Painful Case" as a thematically central story, emphasizing the importance of performance and spiritual selfishness.

Cox, Roger L. "Johnny the Horse in Joyce's 'The Dead.'" *James Joyce Quarterly* 4 (Fall 1966):36–41. Argues that the epiphany of the story is the scene where Johnny circles the statue of King William.

Culler, Jonathan. "The Application of Theory." *James Joyce Quarterly* 18 (1981):287–92. Overview of attempts to apply critical theory to "Eveline."

Daiches, David. *The Novel and the Modern World*. Chicago: University of Chicago Press, 1960. Emphasizes the lyrical, subjective quality of "The Dead," which departs from the objective naturalistic mode of the previous stories.

Deane, Paul. "Motion Picture Techniques in James Joyce's 'The Dead.'" *James Joyce Quarterly* 6 (Spring 1969):231–36. Discusses the rhythm of scenes and sequences in "The Dead" as analogous to cinematic techniques.

Deming, Robert. *A Bibliography of James Joyce Studies*. 2d ed. Boston: G. K. Hall, 1977. Excellent compilation of reviews, critical articles, and primary sources concerning Joyce's writings.

———. *James Joyce: The Critical Heritage*. 2 vols. London: Routledge, 1970. Includes numerous important reviews and essays on *Dubliners*.

Eagleton, Terry. *Literary Theory: An Introduction*. Minneapolis: University of Minnesota Press, 1983. Comprehensible introduction to currents of literary theory that have influenced recent criticism of *Dubliners*.

Eliot, T. S. "Ulysses, Order, and Myth." *Dial* 75 (1923):480–83. Reprinted in *Selected Prose of T. S. Eliot*. Edited by Frank Kermode. New York: Harcourt Brace Jovanovich, 1975. The classic statement of the "mythic method" in fiction.

Ellmann, Richard. *James Joyce*. New York: Oxford University Press, 1982. The standard biography, which includes an extensive discussion of the composition of *Dubliners* and a chapter on "The Backgrounds of 'The Dead.'"

French, Marilyn. "Missing Pieces in Joyce's *Dubliners*." *Twentieth-Century Literature* 24 (1978):443–72. Draws attention to unresolved aspects of the text, particularly the "masking language" that highlights the paralysis of the Dubliners.

Fuger, Wilhelm. *Concordance to James Joyce's "Dubliners."* New York: Olms, 1980. Cross-references verbal echoes.

Fussell, Paul. *The Great War and Modern Memory*. New York: Oxford University Press, 1975. Insightful history of the political and cultural contexts of Joyce's early career.

Garrett, Peter, ed. *Twentieth Century Interpretations of "Dubliners."* Englewood Cliffs, N.J.: Prentice Hall, 1972. Casebook including numerous standard essays of the early period of the Joyce industry.

Garrison, Joseph. "*Dubliners:* Portraits of the Artist as Narrator." *Novel* 8 (Spring 1975):226–40. Argues that the development of the narrative voice in *Dubliners* reflects Joyce's movement toward a more objective aesthetic perspective.

Ghiselin, Brewster. "The Unity of Joyce's *Dubliners*." *Accent* 16 (Spring 1956):75–88. A classic essay identifying the rich symbolic texture, ultimately unified by Christian images and ideas, underlying the realistic details of *Dubliners*.

Gifford, Don. *Joyce Annotated: Notes for "Dubliners" and "Portrait of the Artist."* Berkeley: University of California Press, 1982. Annotates various obscure details.

Goldberg, S. L. *James Joyce*. New York: Grove Press, 1962. Emphasizes Joyce's immaturity at the time he wrote *Dubliners*.

Hart, Clive, ed. *James Joyce's "Dubliners": Critical Essays*. London: Faber,

1969. The best single source of readings of individual stories, including excellent chapters by David Hayman, Zack Bowen, and others.

Hayashi, Tetsumaro. *James Joyce: Research Opportunities and Dissertation Abstracts*. Jefferson, N.C.: McFarland, 1985. Catalogs dissertations written on Joyce, including over a dozen on *Dubliners*.

Heumann, Mark J. "Writing—and Not Writing—in Joyce's 'A Painful Case.'" *Eire-Ireland* 16 (1981):81–97. Emphasizes the self-reflexive implications of Joyce's treatment of Duffy's writing.

Jones, David. "Approaches to *Dubliners*: Joyce's." *James Joyce Quarterly* 15 (Winter 1978):108–18. Identifies and traces the impact of Joyce's early comments on *Dubliners*.

Joyce, Stanislaus. *My Brother's Keeper*. New York: Viking Press, 1958. Memoir including extensive commentary on the composition of Dubliners.

Kaye, Julian. "The Wings of Daedalus: Two Stories in *Dubliners*." *Modern Fiction Studies* 4 (Spring 1958):31–41. Discussion of "An Encounter" and "The Dead," arguing for a more sympathetic view of Stephen Dedalus.

Kelleher, John V. "Irish History and Mythology in James Joyce's 'The Dead.'" *Review of Politics* 27 (July 1965):414–33. Influential presentation and analysis of the presence of Irish history and mythology in "The Dead."

Kenner, Hugh. *Dublin's Joyce*. Boston: Beacon Press, 1962. Discusses the structural progression of *Dubliners* and identifies "The Sisters" and "A Painful Case" as crucial stories.

———. *Joyce's Voices*. Berkeley: University of California Press, 1978. General study of Joyce's canon, including the important stylistic concept of the "Uncle Charles Principle."

Lane, Gary. *A Word Index to James Joyce's "Dubliners."* New York: Haskell House, 1972. Reference work indexing verbal echoes.

Levin, Harry. *James Joyce*. Norfolk, Conn.: New Directions, 1960. Standard introduction to Joyce's career, emphasizing the importance of the city and external realities to the aesthetic of *Dubliners*.

Levin, Richard, and Charles Shattuck. "First Flight to Ithaca: A New Reading of Joyce's *Dubliners*." In *James Joyce: Two Decades of Criticism*, 47–94. Edited by Seon Givins. New York: Vanguard, 1963. Argues that Joyce specifically based *Dubliners* on the *Odyssey*.

MacCabe, Colin. *James Joyce and the Revolution of the Word*. London: Macmillan, 1978. Attempt to synthesize political and psychological theories, combined with an emphasis on *Dubliners'* critique of the privileging of particular perspectives.

Magalaner, Marvin. *Time of Apprenticeship: The Fiction of Young James Joyce*. New York: Abelard-Schuman, 1959. A pioneering study of the composition of *Dubliners*.

Montgomery, Judith. "The Artist as Silent Dubliner." *James Joyce Quarterly* 6 (Summer 1969):306–20. Traces the withdrawal of the narrator(s) of the first three stories into a silence conceived as both protective and liberating.

Morrissey, L. J. "Joyce's Revision of 'The Sisters': From Epicleti to Modern Fiction." *James Joyce Quarterly* 24 (Fall 1986):33–54. Examines Joyce's revisions, noting the development of mature stylistic devices.

Moseley, Virginia. *Joyce and the Bible.* De Kalb, Ill.: Northern Illinois University Press, 1967. Catalogs Joyce's use of the sacraments and rituals of the Catholic Church.

Moyniham, William, ed. *James Joyce's "The Dead."* Boston: Allyn & Bacon Casebook Series, 1965. Casebook including background materials.

Newman, F. X. "The Land of Ooze: Joyce's 'Grace' and *The Book of Job.*" *Studies in Short Fiction* 4 (Fall 1966):70–79. Details allusions and echoes that enrich the symbolic resonance of "Grace."

Olney, James, ed. "Autobiography and the Cultural Moment: A Thematic, Historical, and Bibliographical Introduction." In *Autobiography: Essays Theoretical and Critical,* 3–27. Princeton, N.J.: Princeton University Press, 1980. Historical and theoretical overview of the genre, identifying the significance of *autos, bios,* and *graphia.*

Peake, C. H. *James Joyce: The Citizen and the Artist.* Stanford, Calif.: Stanford University Press, 1977. Emphasizes the tension between engagement and separation throughout Joyce's works.

Pound, Ezra. *Literary Essays.* Norfolk, Conn.: New Directions, n.d. Includes Pound's influential early review of *Dubliners*

Rabaté, Jean-Michel. "Silence in *Dubliners.*" In *James Joyce: New Perspectives,* edited by Colin MacCabe. Bloomington: Indiana University Press, 1982. Insightful reading emphasizing the relationship between "performance" and psychoanalytical motifs.

Reynolds, Mary. *Joyce and Dante: The Shaping Imagination.* Princeton: Princeton University Press, 1981. Detailed study of Dante's influence on Joyce, including an extensive list of verbal echoes and thematic parallels.

Rice, Thomas Jackson. *James Joyce: A Guide to Research.* New York: Garland, 1982. Annotates most significant essays on *Dubliners;* an excellent starting point for research on any topic.

Riquelme, John Paul. *Teller and Tale in Joyce's Fiction: Oscillating Perspectives.* Baltimore: Johns Hopkins University Press, 1983. Employs contemporary theory to explicate the relationship between Joyce's process of discovery and those of the characters within his text.

Rosenberg, Bruce. "The Crucifixion in 'The Boarding House.'" *Studies in Short Fiction* 5 (Fall 1967):44–53. Allegorical reading of plot and character.

Bibliography

San Juan, Epifanio. *James Joyce and the Craft of Fiction*. Rutherford, N.J.: Farleigh Dickinson University Press, 1972. Undistinguished study including readings of each story in *Dubliners*.

Scholes, Robert. "Semiotic Approaches to a Fiction Text: Joyce's 'Eveline.'" *James Joyce Quarterly* 16 (Fall 1978/Winter 1979):65–80. Early attempt to apply critical theory to a story in *Dubliners*.

Scholes, Robert, and Richard Kain. *The Workshop of Daedalus*. Evanston, Ill.: Northwestern University Press, 1965. Anthology including works on which Joyce drew, early drafts of the epiphanies, and a variety of background information.

Scholes, Robert, and A. Walton Litz, eds. *James Joyce's "Dubliners": Text, Criticism and Notes*. New York: Penguin Books, 1976. Text with substantial selection of critical essays.

Scott, Bonnie Kime. *Joyce and Feminism*. Bloomington: Indiana University Press, 1984. Concludes that in *Dubliners* Joyce remains faithful to the actual circumstances of Irish women's lives.

Senn, Fritz. "'The Boarding House' Seen as a Tale of Misdirection." *James Joyce Quarterly* 24 (Summer 1986):405–13. Emphasizes the self-reflexive elements of Joyce's rhetorical strategy and style.

Stone, Harry. "'Araby' and the Writings of James Joyce." *Antioch Review* 25 (Fall 1965):375–410. Identifies numerous structurally and thematically significant allusions to liturgical and literary sources.

Sullivan, Kevin. *Joyce Among the Jesuits*. New York: Columbia University Press, 1958. Study of Joyce's education, including significant information concerning theological influences on his early aesthetic views.

Thelwell, Michael. *Duties, Pleasures, and Conflicts*. Amherst: University of Massachusetts Press, 1987. Includes politically based repudiation of Joyce and modernism.

Torchiana, Donald. *Backgrounds for Joyce's "Dubliners."* Winchester, Mass.: Allen & Unwin, 1986. Compilation of information regarding specific sources and allusions in each of the stories.

Walzl, Florence. "Dubliners." In *A Companion to Joyce Studies,* edited by Bowen and Carens. The best overview of established readings and contextual information on *Dubliners*.

———. "Gabriel and Michael: The Conclusion of 'The Dead.'" *James Joyce Quarterly* 4 (Fall 1966):17–31. Excellent reading of "The Dead," emphasizing recurrent patterns of ambivalent imagery.

———. "*Dubliners:* Women in Irish Society." In *Women in Joyce,* edited by Suzette Henke and Elaine Unkeless, 31–56. Urbana: University of Illinois Press, 1982. Summary of socioeconomic situation of Irish women during Joyce's youth, emphasizing the accuracy of his portrayals.

———. "The Liturgy of the Epiphany Season and the Epiphanies of Joyce."

PMLA 80 (1965):436–50. Influential examination of Joyce's translation of liturgical concepts into aesthetic techniques.

Warren, Robert Penn, and Cleanth Brooks. *Understanding Fiction.* New York: Appleton-Century-Crofts, 1959. Includes a discussion of "Araby" that emphasizes the symbolic and allegorical dimensions of Joyce's style.

Weathers, Winston. "A Portrait of the Broken Word." *James Joyce Quarterly* 1 (Summer 1964):27–40. Discusses Joyce's work as a critique of traditional concepts of communication and language, emphasizing the movement from conversation to monolog in *Dubliners.*

Wilson, Edmund. *Axel's Castle.* New York: Scribner's, 1931. Brief discussion of *Dubliners* as a straight-forward work of naturalistic fiction.

INDEX

Index

Hayman, David, 18
Hemingway, Ernest, 8
Heumann, Mark J., 21
historical themes and approaches, 69–70
Homer, 9; *see Odyssey, Iliad*
Home Rule Movement, 2, 38, 106
Huston, John, 65
Hyde, Douglas, 6

Ibsen, Henrik, 5, 95
Iliad, the, 71
imagism, 13
industrial revolution, 29
Irish Homestead, 8, 35–36
Irish literature, 69; *see also* Irish Literary Renaissance
Irish Literary Renaissance, 1, 5–6
Irish nationalism, 1–3, 38, 58, 104–11; *see* Home Rule Movement, Charles Stewart Parnell, political themes and approaches
"Ivy Day in the Committee Room," 2, 16, 18, 30, 38–39, 42, 45, 93, 95, 99, 103–11

James, Henry, 5, 8
James Joyce Quarterly, 16–17, 20
Jones, David, 12
Joyce, James, comments on *Dubliners*, 11–13; family influences, 1–3; interest in cinema, 65–66; Jesuit education, 79; on socialism, 105; view of Dublin, 33–34, use of Irish literary references, 69

WORKS—PROSE: *Dubliners*, 7–122; *Finnegans Wake*, 7, 9, 11, 15, 19, 27, 86, 99, 101, 103–4, 122; *Portrait of the Artist as a Young Man, A*, 13–14, 16, 30, 49–50, 54, 63; *Stephen Hero*, 8, 48–51, 76; *Ulysses*, 7, 9, 11–15, 17, 19, 27, 30, 32, 85, 91, 99, 104, 122, *see also* entries for individual stories in *Dubliners*
Joyce, John, 65, 75, 79, 100
Joyce, Nora Barnacle, 65, 75–76
Joyce, Stanislaus, 13, 29, 34, 39, 57, 75, 82, 105–6

Kain, Richard, 16, 49
Kaye, Julian, 68
Kelleher, John, 69–70
Kenner, Hugh, 14–15, 18, 46; *see also* Uncle Charles Principle

Lane, Gary, 15
language as theme, 19–20, 42–47, 115–16; *see also* stylistic issues
Larbaud, Valery, 6
Levin, Harry, 13–15, 22–23
Levin, Richard, 14–15, 88–89
Lewis, Wyndham, 6
"Little Cloud, A," 40–41, 47, 81, 90, 94–96, 112–20
Litz, A. Walton, 18
Luther, Martin, 28

MacCabe, Colin, 21–22
Magalaner, Marvin, 16, 18
Mangan, James Clarence, 16
Mann, Thomas, 8
Márquez, Gabriel García, 8
Marx, Karl, 100
marxism, 111–12; *see also* political themes and approaches
men. *See* sexual themes, family themes
modernism, 1, 3–7, 27–33, 102–4, 109, 115, 121–2; *see* imagism
monomyth, 89–90, 98, 103
Montgomery, Judith, 77
Moore, George, 6, 69
Morrissey, L. J., 35

Index

ABOUT THE AUTHOR

A member of the Department of Afro-American Studies at the University of Wisconsin-Madison, Craig Hansen Werner is the author of *Paradoxical Resolutions: American Fiction Since James Joyce* and *Adrienne Rich: The Poet and Her Critics.* He has published essays on a wide range of subjects including William Faulkner, Gwendolyn Brooks, Charles Dickens, David Rabe, Amiri Baraka, and pluralist literary theory. A native of Colorado, he works with the New York based theater-music group Abreaction, which has recently completed work on a recording of the radio play/opera *Game Theory.*